D1480718

WENDEL

My Life in Hockey

BY WENDEL CLARK
WITH SCOTT MORRISON AND JEFF JACKSON

Wendel (left) shares a break at a Leafs practice with Rick Vaive and Russ Courtnall (right).

PERMISSIONS

ISBN: 1-928846-18-1
Printed in Canada

"The King & the Kid" reprinted by permission of Gare Joyce.
"Wendel Clark Muscles into GTA Bar Biz Scene" reprinted by permission of TorStar Syndication Services.
"The Nightmare Off the Ice" reprinted by permission of The St. Petersburg Times.

Photo imaging: Gera Dillon, Toronto, Ont.
Book design: James Wilkins, Birmingham, Ala.
Cover design: Kathleen Doody, Toronto, Ont.
Special front cover graphics: Jackson Creative, Milton, Ont.

Photo Credits:

Graig Abel Photography: Front Cover, 1, 41, 42, 49, 50, 54-all, 55-top, 66-top middle, 66-top right, 72, 73, 74-75, 76, 77, 78, 79, 81, 82.

Wendel Clark Family Collection: 2, 3, 4, 5, 7-top, 7-bottom, 8-all, 9-all, 10, 12, 14-all, 15-both, 16-both, 17-all, 18-all, 19-all, 20-all, 21-all, 22-both, 23-both, 24, 25, 26-both, 27, 28-both, 29, 30-both, 31, 32, 34-both, 35, 38, 40, 43, 44, 45, 46, 47, 48, 55-bottom left, 55-bottom right, 56, 57-both, 58, 59, 60, 61, 62, 63, 64, 65, 66-top left, 66-bottom left, 66-bottom right, 67-both, 68, 69, 70, 71, 86, 89-left, 90, 93, 94-all, 95-all, 96-both, 97-all, 98-both, 99-both, 100-all, 101-all, 102-both, 103-both, 104, 105-both, 106-both, 107-both, 108-all, 109-all, 110-both, 111-both, 113-top, 113-right, 114-top, 114-right, 115-all, 116-all, 117-all, 118-all, 119-all, 120-all, 121-all, 122-all, 123-all, 124-all, 125-all, 126-all.

Hockey Hall of Fame: 89-right.
Jackson Events: 83-both, 84-both, 113-left.
Chuck Kochman: 114-middle.
The Northeast Chronicle: 6-7, 13.
Sylvia Picota: 52, 53, 112.
The Toronto Star: 85.

CONTENTS

Harold Ballard; his dog, Puck, and Wendel share a laugh with Leaf teammates in 1989.

To my parents, Les and Alma, for teaching me my values, responsibility and the meaning of hard work. To Mom for the countless hours she spent in all of those cold town rinks with us three boys and for her trunk loads of memories.

To my brothers, Donn and Kerry, for their love and support.

To the people of my hometown of Kelvington, Sask. – thanks for your support, coaching, teaching and friendship.

To Notre Dame for continuing to instill the values that were started at home. And to Barry Mackenzie and Terry O'Malley. Thanks!

To the Saskatoon Blades, Nate Brodsky, Darryl Lubinicki, Denis Beyak and the rest of the Blades family, Saskatoon players and fans.

Special thanks to my billets, Ray and Nettie Fenner.

To the Toronto Maples Leafs, my second family – from Mr. Ballad, Mr. Stavro, Larry Tanenbaum and Cliff Fletcher, the most respected man in hockey. Thank you!

To the Toronto Maple Leafs staff, players, fans and the Toronto media – thanks for being such a big part of my life. Special thanks to the guy who kept me going all those years – my physical therapist, Chris Broadhurst.

To my dear friend as well as my agent, Don Meehan, the wisest man in hockey. "Good things happen to good people."

To my wife, Denise, and our three children: Kylie, Kassidy and Kody – thanks for being my rock.

Last, but not least, to Andrew Jackson, Scott Morrison, Jeff Jackson and Jennifer Petteplace – thanks for pulling this together.

THIS BOOK IS DEDICATED TO MY FATHER, LES CLARK

Les Clark was born in Wadena, Sask., in 1936 and began farming at the age of 14. As a youngster, he played hockey for teams in Canora, Moose Jaw, Humboldt and Prince Albert. Afterward, he played for the Saskatoon Wesleys of the Saskatchewan Junior Hockey League, then went to the U.S. and played for the Philadelphia Ramblers of the Eastern Hockey League in 1957-58, the Troy Bruins of the International Hockey League in 1957-58 and the Charlotte Clippers of the EHL in 1958-59.

In 1959, he would return to Saskatchewan, where he operated the Kelvington skating rink and coached and played for the Kelvington Wheat Kings. He later became a successful youth hockey coach and a farmer.

In 1961, he married Alma Margarette Pinder and they had three sons: Donn, Wendel and Kerry.

He passed away in January 2009.

BOSTON BRUINS
Lloyd Gronsdahl

26
BARRY MELROSE

JOE KOCUR

CAPTAIN
Wendel Clark

KERRY
CLARK

KELVINGTON
CANADA'S HOCKEY FACTORY

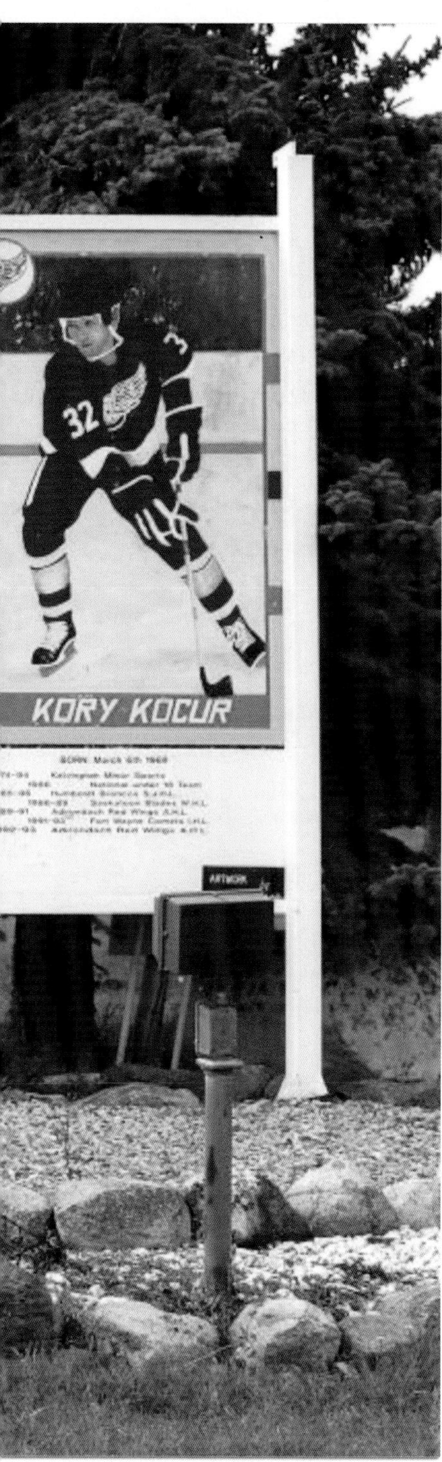

Wendel (right) and his younger brother, Kerry, at Atom League practice in Kelvington, Sask.

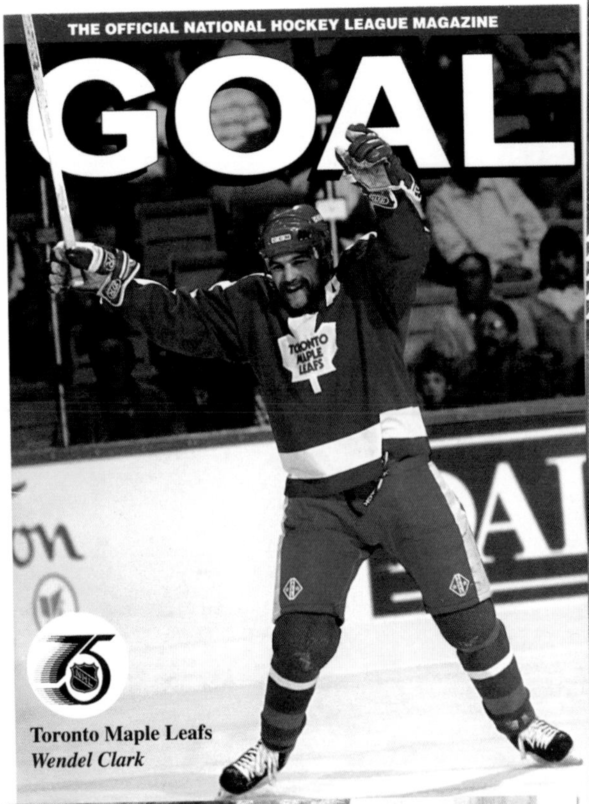
THE OFFICIAL NATIONAL HOCKEY LEAGUE MAGAZINE
GOAL
Toronto Maple Leafs
Wendel Clark

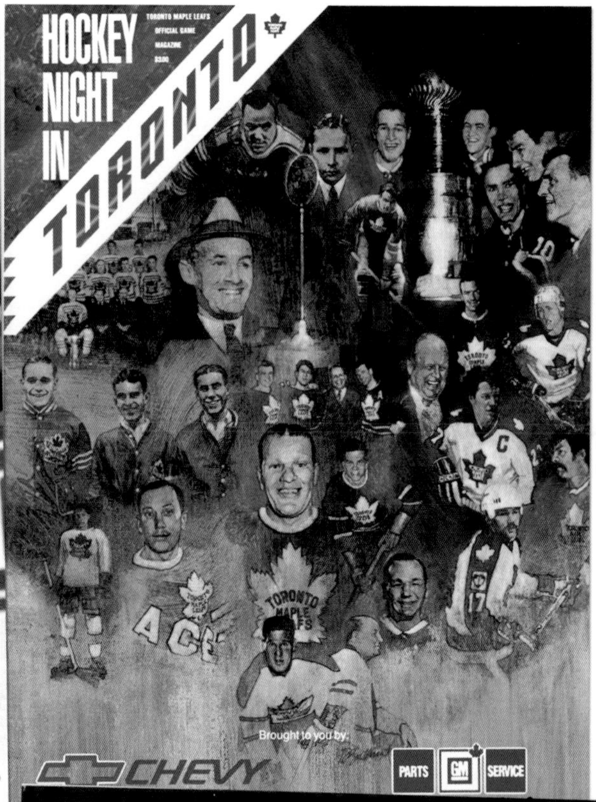
HOCKEY NIGHT IN TORONTO
Brought to you by:
CHEVY
PARTS GM SERVICE

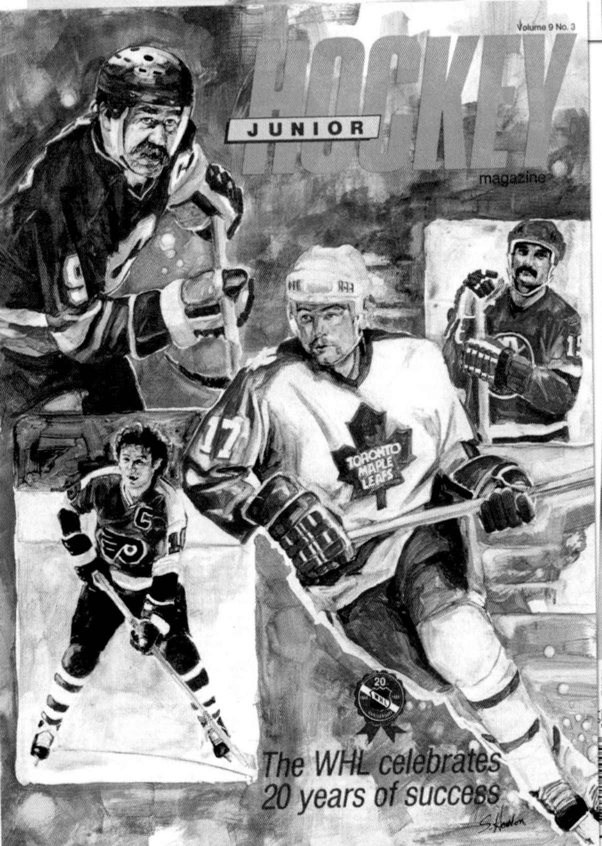
Volume 9 No. 3
JUNIOR HOCKEY
magazine
The WHL celebrates
20 years of success

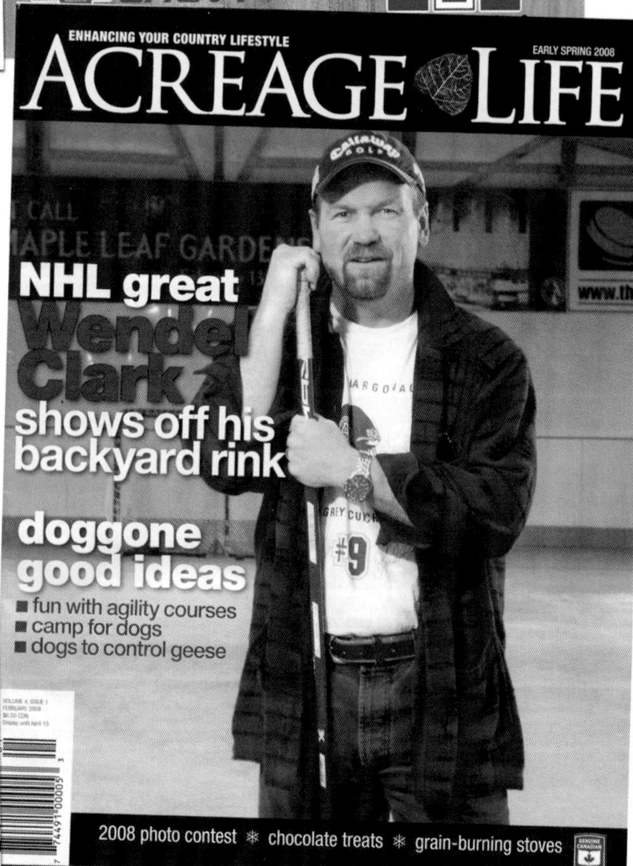
ENHANCING YOUR COUNTRY LIFESTYLE
EARLY SPRING 2008
ACREAGE LIFE
NHL great
Wendel Clark
shows off his backyard rink
doggone good ideas
fun with agility courses
camp for dogs
dogs to control geese
2008 photo contest
chocolate treats
grain-burning stoves

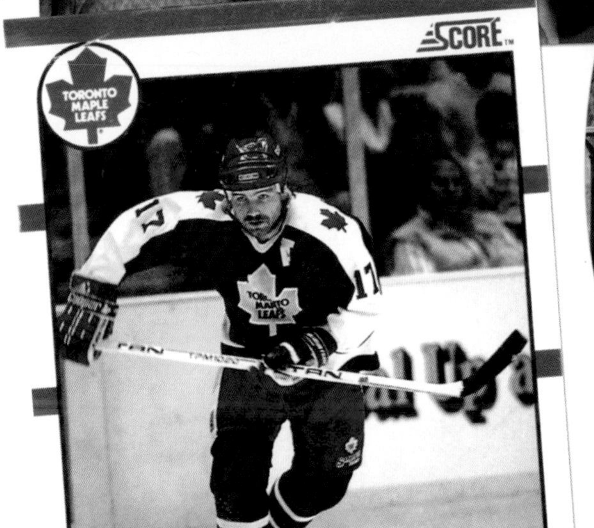

TOP: Wendel autographs a hockey card for a fan at the 1985 NHL Draft. **ABOVE:** The Clarks in 2003.

Wendel and Jeff Jackson (right) at Toronto Maple Leafs practice in 1985.

I first met Wendel in December of 1984 at the tryout camp for Canada's 1985 World Junior team. We didn't meet the way that most people do. I met "Clarkie" when he took me hard into the boards during a simple drill on the first day of camp. I remember thinking to myself, "Who is this guy? And why is he hitting so hard in practice?" In retrospect, the answer to my question was very clear. Wendel was simply being Wendel. He was just trying to get himself noticed; to show he could be a difference maker; to earn a spot on the most prestigious of all junior teams in Canada.

As many of you might already know, that 1985 World Junior team came home from Finland victorious and proudly wearing gold medals around our necks. When I look back at that tournament, there were a lot of very good performances by members of our team, both individually and collectively. But to my mind, one of the most important factors in our success was Wendel's ability to jump off the bench and deliver a devastating body check or score a big goal at the exact moment that we needed it most.

In that tournament, he was versatile, he was tough, he was intense and he was talented. He was also a very humble farm boy who quickly earned the respect and admiration of his teammates. These are all traits that followed him when he made the successful jump to the NHL the next season as a teammate of mine with the Toronto Maple Leafs.

When the Leafs selected Wendel with the 1st overall selection in the 1985 NHL Entry Draft, I was ecstatic. We had become good friends during our time together in Finland and I had seen up close what Wendel could mean to a team. I knew that with Clarkie's arrival in Toronto, the losing culture and attitude around the Leafs was about to be changed for the better.

As a rookie, he took the NHL by storm. As his teammate, it was fascinating to watch as Leaf fans and the entire city of Toronto fell in love with Wendel. Fans loved his western Canadian small-town boy demeanor, his fu manchu moustache and his mullet haircut. Clarkie was absolutely fearless and the Toronto fans immediately identified with his courage and his seemingly limitless willingness to take on all comers. He hit anything that moved, fought most of the League's tough guys and even had time to score 34 goals – not bad for a guy who had only played the odd shift as a forward prior to be drafted by the Leafs.

As we all know, Wendel went on to become Leaf captain on some pretty good Leaf teams in the 1990's. And although he left the Leafs via trade on a couple of occasions, he always returned to a hero's welcome from the Leafs' faithful. This love affair between Leaf fans and Wendel is something that has endured for close to 25 years.

When I was asked if I would write the introduction to this book, I was honoured but at the same time, a little bit nervous. What could I write about a guy who is an iconic sports figure, not only in Toronto, but throughout the entire country?

Having been a teammate of Clarkie's on a couple of different teams and having considered him a good friend for almost 25 years, I can tell you that he is one of the most unique pro sports heroes you would ever meet. He is larger than life, but at the same time about as down to earth as you can get. He is approachable, humble, and without an ounce of pretense or ego. He gives his time generously but quietly to a great number of charitable causes and is a great husband and father to Denise and their three children. The young stars of today could learn a lot from my buddy from Kelvington.

On November 22, 2008, I was fortunate to be in attendance at the Air Canada Centre on the night that the Leafs honoured Wendel by hoisting his Number 17 jersey to the rafters along with other Leaf greats. Prior to the ceremony that night, I happened to run into Clarkie in the corridor outside of the Leaf dressing room. He was standing by himself and looking a little out of sorts. I asked him how he felt and if he was nervous about what was about to take place. He replied that he was as nervous as he had ever been before a game during his career and that he hoped he didn't screw up his acceptance speech.

In typical Wendel fashion, he kept his speech short and to the point. He thanked the fans for their support and they returned the favour by giving him a long and loud ovation, their way of saying thanks for his years of commitment and service to the team they all loved. It was pretty cool to watch and kind of hard to believe that it had been almost 25 years since he walked into Toronto in his cowboy boots and jeans and gave Leaf fans something to feel good about.

Jeff Jackson
Toronto, Ont.
October 28, 2009

Kelvington, Sask.

Canada's Hockey Factory

When you grow up on a farm outside a town of maybe a thousand people like Kelvington, located in the middle of Saskatchewan, you don't really ever think that one day you'll be playing in the National Hockey League. It's not even a boyhood dream.

For a kid in Kelvington, the NHL was just too far away from reality. I guess that's why I never really had a favourite NHL team, although I did have a poster of Bobby Orr on my bedroom wall.

The truth is, for my friends and me hockey was much more fun playing it than watching it. Sure, I liked Bobby Orr, but we didn't get to see a whole lot of the Boston Bruins on TV. Saturday nights, of course, meant "Hockey Night in Canada" and in those days that usually meant Toronto or Montreal games were on TV. The games would come on at 6 p.m. (Saskatchewan time). Our parents would be at home watching, but we were always at the rink. I didn't watch that many NHL games on TV back then.

For a boy growing up in Kelvington the dream was making our local senior team and play in front of the hometown fans on Wednesday and Saturday nights. The guys we really looked up to, and really wanted to be, were the guys right in our own back yard, the guys on the Kelvington senior team. They were our heroes.

For us, Regina and Saskatoon were the big cities in Canada. And so were local towns like Humbolt and Yorkton. Never mind that they had populations of only about 15,000. Places like Toronto or Vancouver or Montreal were never on our radar and neither was the NHL. The plan was to grow up and be a farmer like your Dad and maybe play some senior hockey if you were lucky. That's just the way it was.

For me, the year was divided into two seasons: baseball in the summer and hockey in the winter. Like most towns across Canada, during the winter, the local arena was the centre of attention and activity. That's where the action was. But because there was no ice at the Kelvington Arena until early December, in early November we would start skating and playing some shinny on the frozen ponds, or sloughs as we called them, on the farm.

When the rink finally opened, we would practically live there. The rink was like home for me; seven days a

(Clockwise, beginning with top left) Wendel with Atom League trophies; Kelvington school photo, age 12; with Gramma Prinder, and posing with a new trophy with his Mom.

week – that's where I would be. And because my Dad was in charge of a lot of the minor hockey in town and ran the senior team, too, it allowed me the opportunity to skate with a wide range of different age groups, most of them older. And hockey-wise that helped.

I've often been asked who the biggest influence was on my hockey career. The answer's easy. It was my Dad, Les Clark. When I was young and still at home, he taught me the fundamentals of the game. With Dad, everything was about working hard. It didn't matter whether it was practice or a game; you gave everything you had to the best of your ability every time you stepped on the ice. It was always maximum effort from start to finish. Anything less was letting yourself and your team down.

He always told us, "if you're doing a shooting drill in practice, you shoot to score." He also told us "that you don't just skate all the way down the ice to simply dump the puck into the corner. You always gave it your best." Same thing with passing the puck, he always told us to "pass it like you mean it or you're just wasting time."

Wendel, age 2.

With Dad, nothing was half-way.

And as big as Dad was on going out and being your best, he was probably more of a perfectionist at hockey than anything. He was just as big, and maybe even bigger, on respect.

That applied to hockey and everything else. If there ever was a problem situation involving any of the Clark boys, there was never any question who'd be held responsible or getting the blame; it was which ever one of us was involved. And there would be no sympathy at home. With my Dad, and my Mom for that matter, when it came to people in general and people of authority in particular – teachers, coaches – it was all about respect. When you gave it, you got it. That was my Dad.

One of the best things about being raised on a farm is the freedom you have to do things at such an early age that city kids can't even imagine. For example, I got to drive tractors and trucks and almost anything else on the farm with wheels. I even got my first traffic ticket when I was nine years old.

Dad had taken the tractor to Kelvington for repairs and when it was fixed a few days later, he told me to go to the shop after school and drive the tractor back home instead of taking the school bus. As I was driving the tractor through town, I was stopped by the RCMP. The Mountie and I waited on the side of the road for one of my parents to arrive and drive the tractor back to the farm because he didn't know how to drive it. It was actually my Mom, Alma, who got the ticket.

There were three boys in the Clark family: my older brother, Donn, my younger brother, Kerry, and me. We had the usual fights that most brothers have. Most of the time nothing too serious. But once in a while they could get pretty intense.

WEYBURN'S 14TH ANNUAL PEE WEE 1976 HOCKEY TOURNAMENT

When you're living on a family farm in rural Saskatchewan, (in one direction our nearest neighbours were six miles away), you have to rely on each other for entertainment. There was absolutely no hanging around the house as far as Mom and Dad were concerned. There were no video games and hardly any television. Besides, we could only get two stations. So if you weren't eating, sleeping or working, you were outside playing some kind of sport.

We were also more fortunate than most families. We had lots of relatives living nearby. Actually, about a quarter mile away, which in that part of the province is "next door," is where my cousins – Neil, Darryl and Roy Clark – lived. And since we were all fairly close in age, we would always be playing football, baseball, or hockey together.

I got my first pair of skates when I was the age of two and started playing hockey when I was four or five. At that age, unlike today, there were no organized teams or tryouts. Like most small towns, there were only eight to

TOP: Wendel (Row 1, second from right) and the Kelvington Pee Wee team. **BELOW:** Wendel (Row 2, fourth from left) got his start playing on the Kelvington Lions Atom League team.

(Left to right) Wendel and Dean Harcourt; receiving a Pee Wee trophy, at practice in Kelvington.

The Kelvington Pee Wee team at a hockey tournament in Weyburn, Sask. Wendel is located on Row 1, second from right.

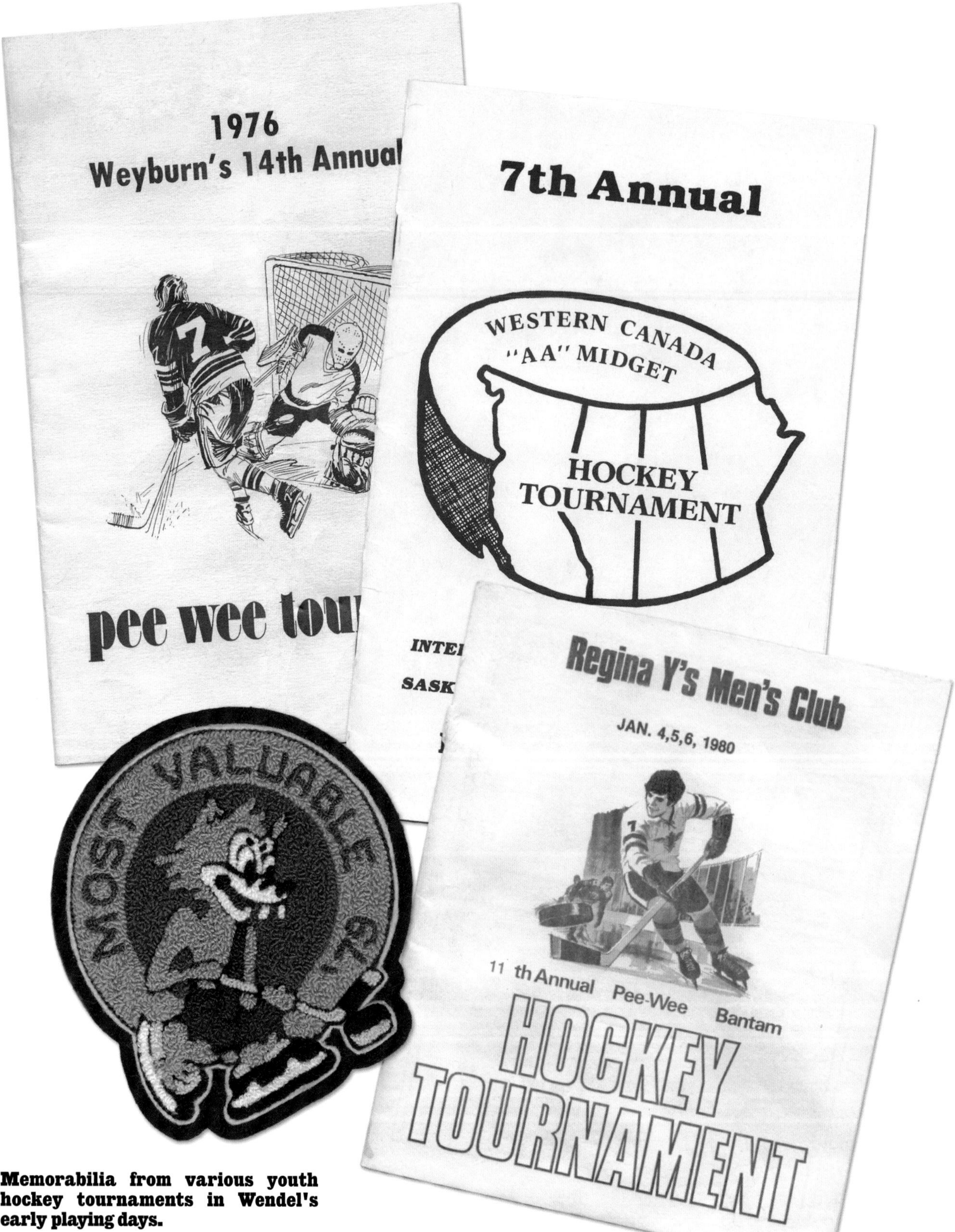

Memorabilia from various youth hockey tournaments in Wendel's early playing days.

12 kids in an age group, so everybody made the team regardless of ability. It was all about fun.

I played defence all through minor hockey and even then I was very physical and offensive-minded. But it wasn't until my first year of Bantam AAA in Yorkton that I actually started to think that maybe I had what it took to get somewhere in hockey. And for me that meant playing Tier Two junior in Yorkton. My older brother, Donn, had played there and, up until then, it was the highest level of hockey I had ever seen live.

Aside from school and the farm, hockey pretty much occupied my every waking hour.

Not only was I on the bantam and midget teams in Kelvington, but I was playing bantam in Yorkton. It was a 200-mile round trip from the farm and either Mom or Dad drove me there, three to five days a week for practice and games. This meant some days I would miss the last two classes of school, go to Yorkton, practice or play in a game, and then we would jump back in the car and head home, arriving at one or two in the morning. I'd try to get a few hours sleep and then be up and ready to catch the bus for school at eight. That was my daily routine for just about the entire winter.

When I was 15 and ready to make the move to midget hockey, there was only one place Mom and Dad wanted me to play – it was at the legendary Notre Dame College at Wilcox, Sask. It was located about 190 miles from Kelvington and with a population of about 100, it was even smaller than Kelvington. Because of its tremendous history of hockey achievements and championships, the Notre Dame Hounds had earned a national reputation.

As a result, it was like a magnet in attracting some of the finest young talent from across the country. My brother, Donn, had attended Notre Dame and really liked the school's hockey program. The school emphasized excellence, not only on the ice but in the classroom. For my parents it was a no-brainer; Notre Dame was the place for me.

At the time, none of us realized that I would probably never live at the family home again.

When you first arrive at Notre Dame nobody really knows anybody. The size of the student body is about 400 and a hundred of them are "elite" hockey players from all across Canada. And they are there for one reason: to make the school's triple-A midget team.

The pressure and the level of competition was like nothing I had ever experienced before. But just like Dad had drilled into me, I gave everything I had, every time I was on the ice. And I guess that's what the coaches wanted to see. Because soon enough, I was a member of the

Wendel's brothers, Donn (left) and Kerry, were also hockey stars in Western Canada.

As a youngster Wendel was a Cub Scout and served as captain of the Kelvington Pee Wee team.

ABOVE: Wendel (Row 3, third from left) and the Notre Dame Hounds celebrate winning the Swift Current Tournament. **BELOW LEFT:** Wendel won the Swift Current Tournament's best defenceman award as a 15-year-old. **BELOW RIGHT:** The next year, at age 16, Wendel won the Swift Current Tournament's best defenceman and MVP awards.

ABOVE: The Kelvington Bantam hockey team. Wendel is located on Row 2, fourth from right.
BELOW: Wendel (far right) was selected to the 1983 Swift Current Tournament All-Star team.

The Notre Dame Hounds at hockey tournaments in 1982 and 1983.

Notre Dame teammates Russ Courtnall (middle) and Gary Leeman (right) challenge Wendel in a game of rock, paper or scissors. This trio would later become the famous "Hound Line" with the Toronto Maple Leafs.

The Clark Family at home in Kelvington, Sask.: (left to right) Don, Les, Wendel, Alma and Kerry.

1981-82 Notre Dame Hounds.

It's a fact that great teams have to have a great coach and we certainly had one in Barry MacKenzie. During his playing days, he'd been on the 1961 Memorial Cup champion St. Michael's Majors. After that he played for Canada's national team, which was coached by Father David Bauer, the legendary junior and Team Canada coach. Barry played in the 1964 and '68 Olympics, then briefly with the Minnesota North Stars, before becoming the Hounds' hockey coach.

In a way, playing for Barry was like playing for my Dad. They both believed in working hard and playing hard to get the most out of your abilities. And they both stressed a physical, "team first" philosophy. And what a team it was at Notre Dame, with guys like Russ Courtnall (my future linemate with the Leafs), another future NHL player, Mitch Messier, and Terry Perkins, who was later drafted by the Quebec Nordiques.

Beyond hockey, Notre Dame also allowed us to learn plenty of life's lessons. For example, there was a real sense of community and togetherness. Kids looked after each other, a "sort of old boy, new boy system." You were encouraged to solve problems on your own, but there was never a feeling of being on your own. If you got to the point where you really needed advice or another perspective or a helping hand, you never had to worry, because there would always be somebody there.

Something else about Notre Dame which I really liked

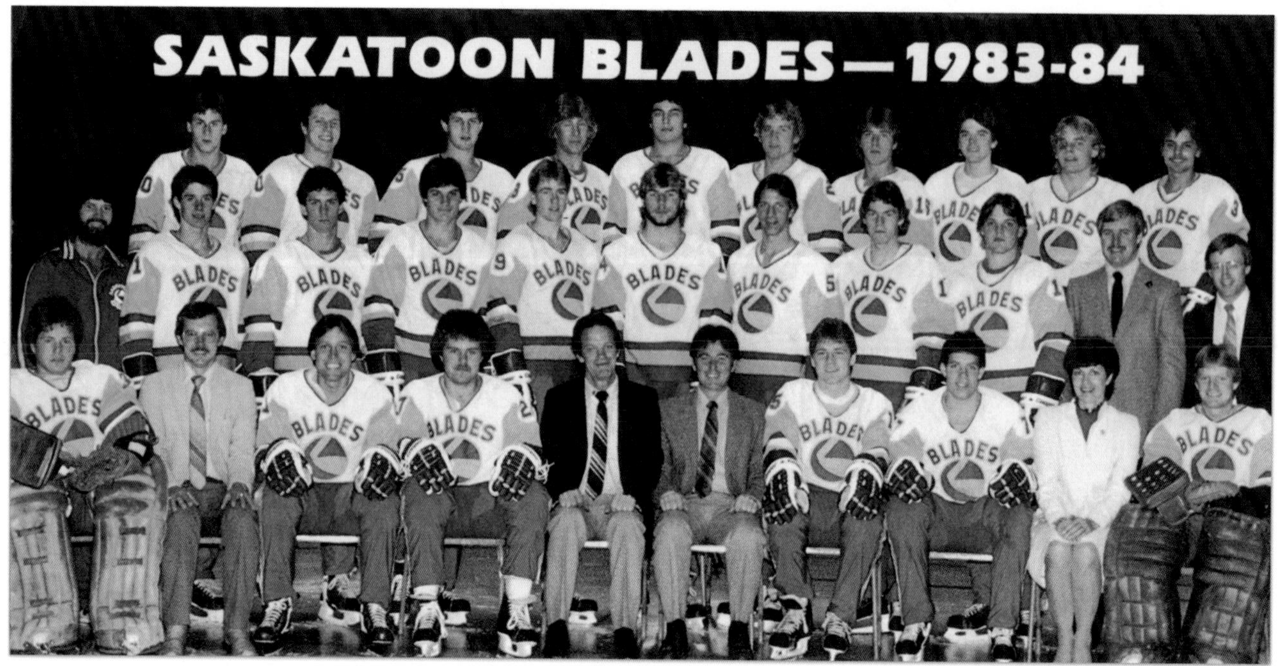

Wendel played for the Saskatoon junior teams in 1983-84 and 1984-85. The future Leafs star is located on Row 1, third from left, on the 1983-84 Blades squad, and on Row 1, second from left on the 1984-85 Blades.

In his second season at Saskatoon (1984-85), Wendel served as the Blades' Alternate Captain.

ABOVE: Wendel is honoured in 1984-85 as a Molson Cup monthly MVP winner. **BELOW:** Bob Bassen (middle) and Wendel (right) receive awards at the junior hockey tournament in Calgary.

was there was no "them" and "us" situation. You know, "us" being the hockey players and "them" being everybody who isn't. No special treatment or free rides just because you were on the school hockey team. And that was especially true when it came to the academics. If you didn't get the grades, then you could forget about hockey. A 50-goal scorer or a fourth-line forward, the rules were the same for everyone.

When I was growing up, there was no Junior draft. I was initially put on the Regina Pats' player list when I was still playing bantam. But they dropped me and my rights were picked up by the Saskatoon Blades.

As crazy as it sounds, I'd been attending junior training camps since I was 13 at Humbolt, Yorkton, Regina and Saskatoon. Even though you knew you weren't going to make the team, you went because of all the ice-time you would get and the chance to play against good hockey players, some as old as 20.

Wendel with his two grandmothers, Gramma Clark (left) and Gramma Pinder (right).

Before returning for my second season at Notre Dame, I was invited to the Saskatoon Blades' training camp – and I made the team.

I was just 16 and I was very excited. However, the excitement didn't last very long. My Dad was out on a combine in one of the fields when he first found out about me making the Blades. He didn't share my excitment to say the least. In fact, he immediately radioed my Mom at the house and told her to "go to Saskatoon, pick him up and take him back to Notre Dame."

I didn't have a clue any of this was happening until Mom arrived at my boarding house in Saskatoon that night. The next thing I knew there I was in Wilcox again and back in my dorm room at Notre Dame.

I was so mad that I didn't call home or talk to my parents for two months. You see, while I'd proven that I was able to play junior A hockey, my Dad wasn't buying it. He felt I would be a lot better off as a player, and as a person, by spending another year with the Hounds.

Once again, Notre Dame had an outstanding team and an outstanding coach in Terry O'Malley, who coached me in that second year.

Like I said, it took me a long time to get over the whole thing, that's how upset I was. In my mind, playing midget for Notre Dame, when I could be playing for Saskatoon, made no sense whatsoever. I guess I felt the same way most teenagers do when their parents won't let them do something they really want to do.

But in hindsight my Dad was absolutely right and I was absolutely wrong. Dad knew that at Notre Dame I'd play 40 minutes a game and be on the ice in every key situation. But as a 16-year-old rookie on a veteran team in Saskatoon, maybe I'd play 10 minutes a game if I was lucky.

Also, I always played a physical, aggressive game and there was no way I was going to change. In junior I'd be up against guys who were practically men. And they weren't going to put up with a 16-year-old running all over the ice and hitting anything that moved. There'd be a price to pay, which, of course, meant dropping the gloves. The truth is, I'd never had a single fight in midget and Dad didn't want me having to go toe-to-toe with some 20-year-old enforcer every night.

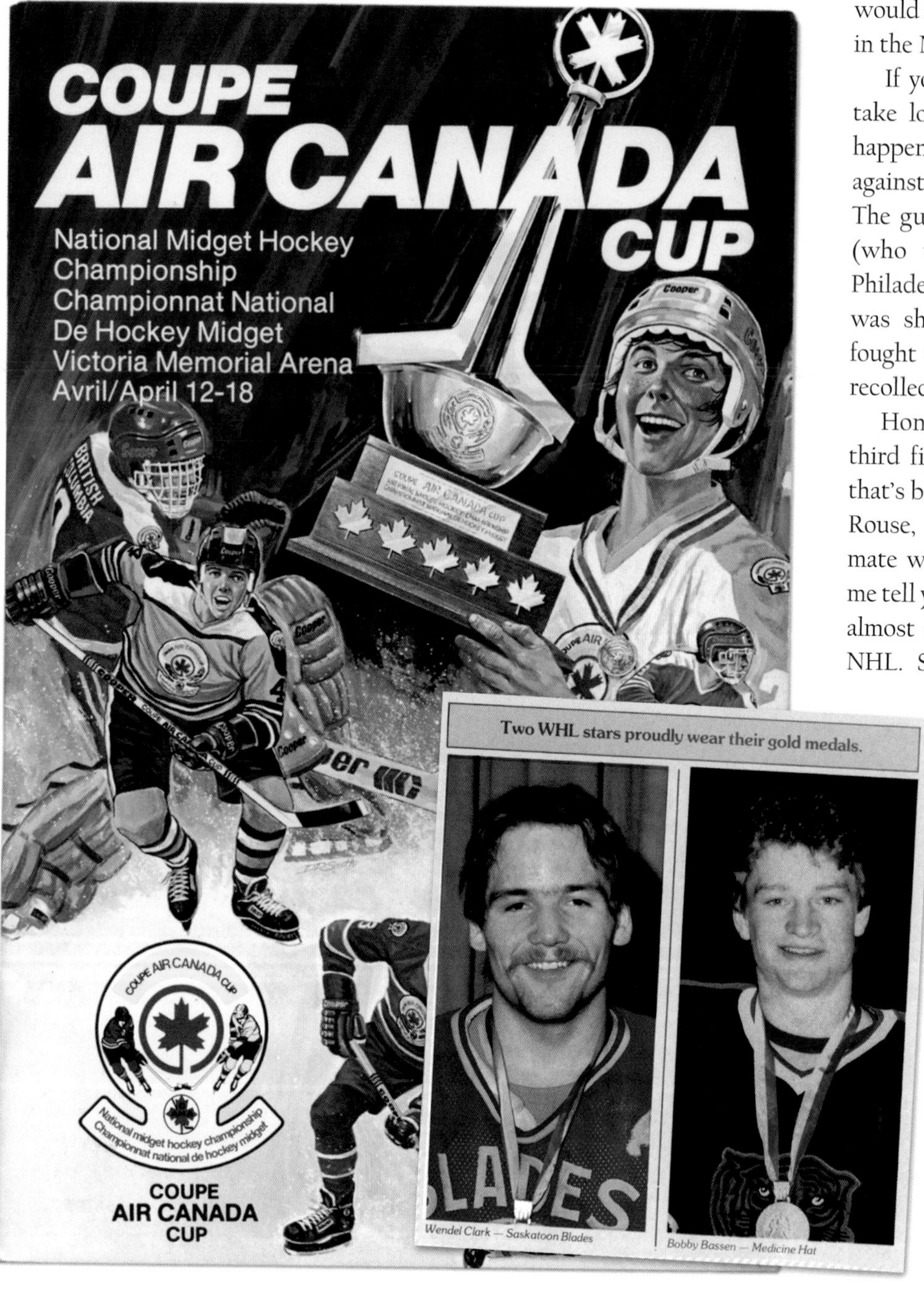

would later go on to a long career in the NHL.

If you're wondering, it didn't take long for my first fight. It happened in my first junior game against the Medicine Hat Tigers. The guy's name was Al Conroy (who would later play with Philadelphia in the NHL). He was short and stocky and we fought twice. To the best of my recollection I did alright.

Honestly, I remember my third fight a lot clearer. Maybe that's because it was against Bob Rouse, who later was a teammate with the Maple Leafs. Let me tell you, back in junior he was almost as big as he was in the NHL. So it's possible he won that fight. I know for sure, Bob was a much better guy to be around when he was with you than when he was against you.

And speaking of tough guys, I should mention that our tough guy on the Blades was my cousin from Kelvington, Joey Kocur, who later had some very good years with the Detroit Red Wings. He was the most feared guy in our league and was the toughest I ever saw.

At least, not yet, because he knew that I was simply wasn't physically ready. So I returned for a second season at Notre Dame and they were two of the best years of my life.

The following fall, in September 1983, at age 17, I was with the Saskatoon Blades to stay, a rookie on a young team, anchoring the defence with Trent Yawney, who

In Saskatoon, Joey looked after the guys who needed to be looked after. And since he knew I could handle myself, I wasn't one of them. I had my fair share of battles that season. Even though I was only 17 and 5-foot-10, 170 pounds, my style of play constantly got me into trouble.

It seemed that I played the whole season with my eyes

With his father (third from left) watching, Wendel receives a hug from his Mom at a ceremony in Saskatoon honouring his successful junior career.

blackened. Since my eyes weren't used to getting punched, they always seemed to be black from the bruises. That first season with the Blades, I wound up with 225 penalty minutes, along with 23 goals and 68 points. The next season I had 32 goals, 87 points and 253 penalty minutes.

People always talk about the grueling travel in the Western league. Truthfully, it's just something we've all grown up with in Western Canada. For most of us, it started in minor hockey where we'd play all over the province and some trips would be eight hours in one direction. And as you move up the ranks, the travel just keeps getting longer and longer.

When you finally make it to junior you're pretty much used to it.

When I was at Saskatoon, our longest trip would be out to the West Coast for games against Victoria and Seattle. We're talking about traveling thousands of miles and a week on the road away from home. And back then there was no television on the buses or video games. Maybe you'd do homework or read a book or whatever it took to kill the time. And all of this on a bus with makeshift beds and a washroom that didn't work half the time.

I can remember the worst trip we had. We had lost all of our West Coast games, including the final one in Seattle. After that game, we had our customary team meal not knowing it would be our last until we got home – 26 non-stop hours later.

Despite the tremendous amount of travel, my first year I only missed 11 days of school. On the shorter trips, you'd leave on Friday and play that night and again on Saturday and Sunday, then bus home. Depending on where we played, you'd arrive back in Saskatoon at around six or seven on Monday morning, grab some breakfast and then head to school.

But I never complained. I loved what I was doing and I loved my life as a hockey player.

Wendel would play on both defence and as a forward for Team Canada at the 1985 World Junior Hockey Championship, which was played at Helsinki, Finland.

The Road to FINLAND

The 1984-85 season was obviously a huge year in my hockey life. It was my draft year so I needed to perform well. After watching Canada's World Junior team win a gold medal in 1982, I was really hoping to get an invitation to try out for the 1985 team. Even though I was being projected to be a fairly high pick in the NHL Draft in June, I knew that the World Junior Team was usually made up of 19-year-olds who had already been drafted by an NHL team the prior year. If I even wanted to think about getting invited to the selection camp, let alone making the team, I needed to make sure I had a strong start with my Western Hockey League team, the Saskatoon Blades.

Fortunately for me, things worked out well early in the season. I was playing close to 40 minutes a game in Saskatoon and in the first couple months of the season, I think I was leading all defencemen in the WHL in scoring. When I got the word in early November that I was going to be invited to the tryout camp in December, in Belleville, Ont., I was really happy. But as much as I was hoping for it, I was still surprised to get the invitation. When it arrived, it seemed so far from reality and I had no idea if I even had a chance to make the team or not.

Like I said, this team normally didn't include undrafted players on its roster. But I was determined to find a way onto that plane headed for Finland and the World Junior Championships.

In early December, before I left for the camp, I got some good advice from my GM at Saskatoon, Darryl Lubiniecki. He told me that the team was going to be looking for a couple of offensive-minded defenseman and that if I expected to have any chance at all of making the team, it was going to be because of my offence. Once I got to the camp in Belleville and into the scrimmages and the exhibition games we played against the Hamilton Steelhawks, in Hamilton, and the Ottawa 67's, in Ottawa, I stuck with that plan and played a pretty high-risk offensive game, taking a lot more chances that I normally would have while playing for the Blades.

Having said that, I didn't totally abandon playing the very physical game I was used to.

Lucky for me, I scored a couple of goals and had a couple of big hits in the two exhibition games. And as a result, I felt pretty good about how I had played at the camp. Still, like all of the other players at the camp, I was sitting on pins and needles as the final cuts were about to be made.

The night before the final team was going to fly to Europe, there was a big meeting with all of the remaining candidates and the team's management and coaches. We were staying at a hotel in Ottawa at this point, having finished playing against the 67's. In that meeting, we were all told to go to bed and get a good night's sleep. The plan was if you didn't get a call early the next morning, then you had made the team. In other words, if your phone rang bright and early, then you were likely taking a plane or a bus back to your junior team instead of the flight to Finland.

Sure enough, the next morning I got the dreaded call to go to Coach Terry Simpson's room to meet with him and Sherry Bassin, the team's General Manager. I remember making my way down the long hotel corridor and being really disappointed since I thought I was about to be sent back to Saskatoon.

Surprisingly, Sherry Bassin started off the meeting by asking me if I would have any problem if the coaches decided to play me at left wing (on offense) instead of on defense. Terry then asked me if I thought I could handle getting a lot less ice time than I was used to getting in Saskatoon.

At this point, I was shocked because I quickly realized that maybe I wasn't being cut after all. I also realized that I hadn't answered any of their questions.

In an effort to respond, I think I blurted out: "I would be happy to be the team's trainer if it meant I was going to Finland."

I can still hear Terry Simpson's voice saying, "Well you're on the team then – but under one condition ... you

ABOVE: The 1985 World Junior Champions from Canada. Wendel is located on Row 2, second from right. BELOW: After the 2-2 tie with Czechoslovakia, Wendel and two teammates celebrate winning junior hockey's greatest prize.

have to get your hair cut before we go to Finland."

When I arrived for training camp, I had pretty long hair – I believe it's referred to as a mullet nowadays – but I think I would have shaved my head if it meant getting on that plane. Needless to say, when I climbed on the team bus later that morning to travel to Mirabel Airport in Montreal, I had found a barbershop.

The team, which included less than 30 people when you counted up all the players, coaches, management and staff, assembled in Montreal and waited to catch a late night flight to Finland. As a group of teenagers, for most of us, this was our first trip to Europe. I think we were all both nervous and excited at the same time. We were going to be away from our families for Christmas and we would have to bond together very quickly in order to make our trip a successful one. In 1982, we had all watched the Team Canada junior squad win the gold medal in 1982 in Rochester, Minnesota, and we wanted to be the first Canadian junior team to win a gold medal on European soil.

Before the 1985 Team Canada squad left to fly to Finland, Wendel was told by his coach to find a local barber shop and get his mullet hair cut.

I really don't remember much about the plane ride to Finland other than Sherry Bassin coming around the plane and showing each of us his big championship ring which he received for being part of the '82 gold medal-winning team. I remember thinking that I would really like to have one of those myself to show off to the boys back in Saskatoon.

As we would soon find out, Sherry was a master at using every method he could to inspire us to return to Canada as champions.

When we landed in Finland, we immediately boarded two buses and headed south to the Vierumäki Olympic training centre, where we would stay for the next few days. The plan was that we would train as a team and try to get to know each other much better, both on and off the ice. Getting to know each other at Vierumäki wasn't too difficult since we were either training at the rink together or hanging out in our log cabins playing poker and trying to find ways to take all of Claude Lemieux's money.

One of the most memorable things about our time at Vierumäki was how really bad the food was. I especially remember how our entire team bonded together over our common dislike of what we were served for breakfast each morning.

What Canadian boy in his right mind would enjoy cold sardines, half cooked eggs and cold cuts every morning at the crack of dawn?

By about the third day, I was dying for steak and eggs and toast.

Despite these meals tasting really bad, my teammates and I still managed to have a lot of laughs while at the same time having some productive on-the-ice workouts over the next few days.

Our coaches' goal after we arrived at Vierumäki was to try and take 20 players – many of whom did not know each other at all – and force us to become friends and teammates in the short time frame before the tournament stated. Their plan worked because when we left Vierumäki, we were a real team.

Our first game of the tournament was against Sweden at the big rink in Helsinki. I'm not afraid to say it: Yes, we were pretty nervous about playing the Swedes after having watched them skate and zip the puck around at one of their practices a week earlier at Vierumäki.

But we were representing Canada on a world stage and none of us wanted to let our country down by losing the first game of the tournament. Our coaches' game plan was to have us play our own style; we had plenty of guys who could score and we wanted to combine that with hard hitting, in-your-face Canadian hockey.

That was fine with me. Our game plan worked per-

1985 JOURNEY TO THE CHAMPIONSHIP

DATE	OPPONENT	VENUE	SCORE
Dec.23	Sweden	Helsinki	8-2
Dec. 25	Poland	Turku	12-1
Dec. 26	West Germany	Helsinki	6-0
Dec. 28	United States	Turku	7-5
Dec. 29	USSR	Turku	5-0
Dec. 31	Finland	Helsinki	4-4
Jan. 1	Czechoslovakia	Helsinki	2-2

WORLD JUNIOR CHAMPIONSHIPS ALL-STAR TEAM

POSITION	PLAYER	TEAM
Goalie	Timo Lehkonen	Finland
Defenceman	Bobby Dollas	Canada
Defenceman	Mikhail Tatarinov	USSR
Forward	Mikko Makela	Finland
Forward	Michal Pivonka	Czechoslovakia
Forward	Esa Tikkanen	Finland

IIHF DIRECTORATE AWARDS

POSITION	PLAYER	TEAM
Forward	Michal Pivonka	Czechoslovakia
Defenceman	Vesa Salo	Finland
Goalie	Craig Billington	Canada

fectly as we outskated, outhit and outscored the Swedes by a score of 8-2. During the third period of that game, I could feel our team gaining a lot of confidence and at that point, I started to really believe that we had the right group of guys to win the tournament.

On Christmas Eve, we had a day off. And since our families were all back home in various parts of Canada, we decided to exchange joke gifts amongst the players, coaches and staff. We had a big dinner together and then did our gift exchanges. And once again, while it seems like it may not have meant much, it was just another way for our team to bond and feel like family.

We played the next two games on Christmas Day, against Poland, and on Boxing Day (December 26th) against Germany. I think we outscored these two teams by something like 18-1.

Having this big of a goal differential was really important in the round-robin format of the tournament. It also allowed the coaches to experiment with different line combinations and positions and in these two games, I started the games on defense but also found myself playing left wing at various times.

I didn't mind that at all. In fact, I kinda enjoyed having a bit more freedom to jump into the offense or go for a big hit while playing forward. It also gave me some needed confidence that if the coaches wanted to use me at forward at some point later in the tournament, I wouldn't disappoint them.

As it turns out, it didn't take that long for the coaches to start playing me more at wing than on defense. In our next game against the U.S., I played mainly up front with only a couple of shifts thrown in on the back end. I had a couple of good hits against that cocky group from the United States and boy, did it feel great when I stepped out of the penalty box and went in on a breakaway and scored. That goal took the air out of the U.S. squad, who at that point in the game actually had us a bit on the ropes. We ended up winning, 7-5, but we certainly had a bit of a scare. Looking back, I'm sure that we had underestimated the U.S. team and made the mistake of looking past them to the crucial matchup of the tournament against the USSR.

Our team had no problem getting fired up for the Russians, who were the pre-tournament favourite.

But just in case we didn't, Sherry Bassin gave one of his famous pre-game speeches and when we went out for the warm-up, our adrenaline had us all pumped beyond belief. We were so wired that a bunch of the guys were screaming over at the Russians that we were "going to kill them." Shayne Corson and Danny Gratton then took turns firing pucks at their skates as they skated by.

You could tell by the look in the Russians' eyes that they didn't know what to expect from us.

We, however could smell blood.

You have to remember that back in 1985, there were really no Russians playing in the NHL yet. They were still our mortal hockey enemies. We had a big hate on for the Big Red Machine. And our team that year in Finland had more than its fair share of guys who loved to play a physical game. Claude Lemieux, Shayne Corson, Jeff Jackson, Bobby Bassen, Jim Sandlak and me. We all enjoyed knocking a guy on his butt as much as scoring a goal.

Once the game started, we came out playing a very physical game and set the tone early on. We really had them looking over their shoulders when we jumped out to an early 1-0 lead in the game.

When I look back at it, I have to agree that my big hit on Mikhail Tatarinov early in the second period probably put a nail in their coffin that day.

Tatarinov was the USSR's top defenseman and he loved to carry the puck. I caught him with his head down at center ice and it was probably one of the best hits of my career. Every once in a while, you deliver a bodycheck where the timing is just right and this just happened to be one of those times. Tatarinov's gloves, stick and helmet were all over the ice and he ended up being knocked unconscious.

After that, the Russian team wasn't the same and we went on to win, 5-0.

I will never forget the feeling of standing on the blue line with my teammates after that game, watching the Canadian flag being raised up to the rafters as "O Canada" was played and we sang our hearts out. That's right, a bunch of macho teenage hockey players were singing together like there was no tomorrow. We had just defeated our most feared opponent and we were enjoying every second of it. It has been fun to watch over the years as other Canadien teams continue this practice of singing our national anthem after victories.

After that emotional Russian game, our coaches kept us focused on the fact that we *still* had two big games left to play before we could really celebrate.

First, we had to face the Finns, who were playing in front of their hometown crowd. By this point in the tournament, Terry Simpson was using me mainly at forward. In this game, I don't think I saw a lot of ice time as we were shorthanded for a good part of the game. I remember it was a pretty physical game, with the Finns not backing down an inch. And though we had the lead for much of the contest, it ended in a 4-4 tie.

The fact that I didn't play a lot in this big game didn't really bother me at all. I knew this might happen at some point in the tournament. In our final game against the Czechs, we would only need a tie against them to win the gold medal. And that was the only thing me and my

Wendel battles for the puck along the boards during the 1985 World Junior Championship.

teammates were thinking about at that point.

As we prepared for the Czechs, I wouldn't say we were overconfident. How could we be when they had the exact same record as we did? I think the fact that the Czechs needed an outright win to beat us for the gold helped us all feel really good about our chances.

As a team, we hadn't lost a game yet and we weren't about to let that happen in the biggest game of our lives. We all knew that this was a game we would never forget, win or lose. But just in case, Sherry Bassin gave us another one of his inspirational speeches prior to the game and reminded us all that very few people ever get a chance to be a world champion. For most of us, this was that one opportunity.

At this point in the tournament, our defense was very banged up and Coach Simpson informed me that he was switching me back to defense for this game. I had enjoyed playing up front the last few games with Bobby Bassen and Jim Sandlak and we had played pretty well as the fourth line. But defense was my natural position so I had no problem at all making the switch back and was just happy that I would have a chance to play a part in such an important game.

This was perhaps the most important game I ever played in as a player. Period. But oddly, there is a lot about this game I just don't have a clear recollection of. I remember the final result but the specific details of the game are a bit sketchy.

What I do remember, however, was that we had a whole bunch of good scoring chances but by midway through the third period, we were down by a goal with less than ten minutes left to play.

We were now starting to get desperate about getting one more goal to even up the game.

That's when Terry Simpson called out my name and informed me that I was taking a shift on left wing with Adam Creighton and Brian Bradley, our two leading scorers in the tournament. We went out for a faceoff in the Czech's end and I was instructed by Adam to flip flop positions with "Brads." I did as I was told and the next thing I knew, we had won the face off and Brian had control of the puck to the right of the goalie.

Not really being familiar with where I should be going – I was a defenseman after all – I just tried to get myself open and watch for a rebound. Before I knew it, Brads made a perfect pass right to my stick and I one-timed the

1985 WORLD JUNIOR CHAMPIONSHIP

NO.	PLAYER	HT.	WT.	HOMETOWN	1984-85 TEAM
				Goalies	
1	Craig Billington	5'10"	155	London, ON	Belleville, OHL
30	Norm Foster	5'7"	175	Vancouver, BC	Michigan State
				Defencemen	
2	Brad Berry	6'2"	190	Bashaw, AB	North Dakota
3	John Miner	5'11"	187	Regina, SK	Regina, WHL
5	Bobby Dollas	6'3"	210	Montreal, QC	Winnipeg, NHL
7	Selmar Odelein	6'1"	201	Quill Lake, SK	Regina, WHL
19	Yves Beaudoin	5'9"	180	Pointe-aux-Trembles, QC	Shawinigan, QMJHL
25	Jeff Beukeboom	6'4"	210	Lindsay, ON	Sault Ste. Marie, OHL
				Forwards	
6	Wendel Clark	5'10"	170	Kelvington, SK	Saskatoon, WHL
8	Brian Bradley	5'9"	163	Kitchener, ON	London, OHL
9	Shayne Corson	6'2"	185	Barrie, ON	Hamilton, OHL
10	Greg Johnston	6'1"	205	Barrie, ON	Toronto, OHL
11	Adam Creighton	6'5'	205	Welland, ON	Buffalo, NHL
12	Jeff Jackson	6'1"	190	Dresden, ON	Hamilton, OHL
14	Bob Bassen	5'10"	180	Calgary, AB	Medicine Hat, WHL
16	Dan Hodgson	5'11"	175	Ft. Vermillion, AB	Prince Albert, WHL
21	Claude Lemieux	6'1"	208	Montreal, QC	Verdun, QMJHL
23	Stéphane Richer	6'2"	185	Ripon, QC	Granby, QMJHL
24	Dan Gratton	6'0"	182	Brantford, ON	Oshawa, OHL
26	Jim Sandlak	6'3"	202	Kitchener, ON	London, OHL

TOURNAMENT FINAL RANKINGS

TEAM	GP	W	L	T	PTS.	GF	GA
Canada	7	5	0	2	12	44	14
Czechoslovakia	7	5	0	2	12	32	13
USSR	7	5	2	0	10	38	17
Finland	7	4	1	2	10	42	20
Sweden	7	3	4	0	6	32	26
USA	7	2	5	0	4	23	37
Germany	7	0	6	1	1	9	44
Poland	7	0	6	1	1	10	59

puck past their goalie, Dominik Hasek.

I have to admit that I was as surprised as anyone that my shot had gone in but boy did I feel awesome. I also knew the gold medal was ours if we could hang on for the tie – which we did. Winning a gold medal at such a prestigious tournament is something that my teammates and I are all still very proud of. Sure, many of us went on to have careers in the NHL and a few even won Stanley Cups. But that group of guys on that team in Finland was special, and when we won the gold medal for Canada on New Year's Day 1985, we cemented a lifelong brotherhood that will never fade away.

Twenty-five years later, I sometimes still can't believe that I was even selected to be on that team, let alone be fortunate enough to score the gold medal-winning goal. It meant a lot to me back in 1985 and probably means even more to me now.

Thank God, I was able to find a barber shop that morning in Ottawa or I may have never been allowed on the plane to Finland.

NO. 1

WENDEL CLARK IS, WHAT ABOUT THE MAPLE LEAFS?

TORONTO MAPLE LEAFS

LEAFLAND
Centre of the Hockey World

When you are playing in Toronto and the Maple Leafs are winning, there is no better place to be.

I was the first player taken overall in the 1985 Entry Draft by the Leafs – and that began a memorable nine-year run in Toronto and big changes in my life. My signing bonus was $175,000 Canadian and I didn't even have a bank account!

As previously mentioned, I had spent most of my teenage years on buses traveling around Western Canada in junior hockey. And then, of course, there was the gold medal at the World Junior Championship in Finland.

Wendel is introduced by Joe Bowen at a Leafs luncheon.

But my first season in Toronto was truly something else. Exciting, yes, but also a real eye-opener and a total wake-up call.

My early years with the Leafs were disappointing and frustrating because we kept spinning our wheels. We couldn't win, at least not consistently.

We did, however, enjoy a brief taste of success in the 1986 and 1987 playoffs and it showed us just how good life could be when you are winning in Toronto.

Sometimes as players, there are factors that are simply beyond your control. And frequently, one of them is the front office. It's a player's responsibility to perform at the highest level every time they hit the ice. That's something all of us can control and should be accountable for. But you can't control what is happening above you.

We hit rock-bottom during the 1990-91 season. We finished dead last in the Norris Division with a record of 23-46-11 and there didn't seem to be a whole lot of light at the end of the tunnel.

That is until that summer, on July 1, 1991, to be precise, when Cliff Fletcher arrived as the Leafs new president and general manager. Almost overnight his impact was felt throughout the organization.

Cliff was a winner and one of the most respected men in the game. He won a Stanley Cup with the Calgary Flames in 1989. Within hockey circles, he was admired for his knowledge, integrity and professionalism. He was a straight-shooter. He brought direction, stability and leadership. Most of all, Cliff brought hope.

Personally speaking, all I can say is, his effect on me was immediate and permanent.

That fall, at the Hot Stove Lounge in Maple Leaf Gardens, he made me the 13th player to be captain of the Leafs. It was humbling and overwhelming at the same time. It's hard to describe the feeling of such an honour. And to this day, it ranks as one of the most memorable moments of my career and my life.

Despite the optimism we had, that our fortunes were about to change under Cliff's guidance, that first season was still pretty tough. Once again we missed the playoffs, but we did show signs of improvement and there was that feeling of hope because we all believed in Cliff.

The truth is, even though we struggled somewhat, Cliff had already started putting his fingerprints on the team that season. He had a plan and slowly, but surely, he

ABOVE: Cliff Fletcher, who led Calgary to the 1989 Stanley Cup championship, was the architect of the Leafs' revival in the early 1990's, where they reached the Cup semi-finals twice.

was executing it. He brought in Grant Fuhr and Glenn Anderson from Edmonton, Ken Baumgartner from the Islanders and Mark Osborne from Winnipeg.

And then came the biggie. On January 2, 1992, he made the 10-player trade with the Flames. We got Jamie Macoun, Ric Nattress, Rick Walmsley, Kent Manderville and the key piece of the deal, Dougie Gilmour, who would establish himself as one of the best and most popular players in Leafs history.

For Cliff it was imperative that his best players were also good character guys because that would mean they could control the dressing room and stop, at the very first sign, any potential problems. When guys get disgruntled, divisions and cliques can develop within the team. And that spells big trouble and in a hurry. However, if your key guys are on top of things and are never part of the problem, then chances are they'll make sure there's a fast and effective solution.

One of a coach's biggest challenges is to convince his players to buy what he's selling. In other words, the role the coach has designated for each player is a role that player accepts and is willing to perform night after night, for the good of the team. That was the case with our teams in 1992-93 and 1993-94 and part of it was because of the leadership within the dressing room, a lot of it acquired in the big trade. This is another reason why we were able to turn things around so quickly.

Checking your ego at the door isn't easy. But accepting and perfecting a "role player" position on the roster, can not only extend your career, but it can also make you an integral part of a winning team. Maybe the best examples of that are Kris Draper and Kirk Maltby of the Detroit Red Wings. They're rarely in the spotlight, but they do their jobs, they do whatever they're asked to do for the good of the team. All they've got to show for it is the appreciation and respect of their coaches and teammates – and four Stanley Cup championships.

Obviously, getting Dougie was huge and another big step towards becoming a legitimate Stanley Cup contender. We all felt we were suddenly at the next level. The funny thing is, some people initially didn't realize how good Dougie was, how big it was to get him. Because he'd played in St. Louis and Calgary, his career was generally off the radar. But let me tell you, as players we knew exactly how good Dougie was and what he brought. Dougie was a difference-maker, who was capable of taking us to the next level and we all knew it.

Doug Gilmour was the classic case of a 170-pounder who played like he was 225. Dougie would be the first to admit that he wasn't the most naturally talented player. But nobody ever got more out of himself or gave more of himself than Dougie did. His hockey smarts, heart, determination, intensity – they were all completely off the chart. I'm not sure I've ever been around a guy who was more competitive than him. He simply didn't know the meaning of quit. And he wasn't a "me" guy either, which some stars are. There was never any selfish, prima donna stuff with Dougie. It was always "team" and "teammates" first. He loved to be good on the ice, but he loved for everybody else on the Leafs to be good, too.

Until he came to the Leafs, I'd never been on a team with a centre of Dougie's caliber since my first Canada Cup training camp back in 1987, with guys like Wayne Gretzky, Mario Lemieux, Steve Yzerman and Dale Hawerchuk. And obviously that was only for a couple of weeks.

For some reason we never actually played all that much together during the regular season. That, however, changed in the 1993 playoffs. And because Dougie was so darned good, I had to change, too. Like making sure I was always paying attention to where he was and what he was doing. Because the special ones, like him, make a habit of doing the unexpected, just because they can.

Being a shooter, I like to find holes where you know you can get the shot away. A lot of centres will see you on the ice and if there's a guy standing beside you, they won't pass you the puck. In their eyes, you're covered. But not so with elite centres like Dougie. They just instinctively know that if they put the puck on your stick, then you've got a shot. They know you may be getting checked, but your stick is open. It's the little things like that, which separate the good ones from the great ones. They can create unexpected scoring opportunities

LOEWS WESTBURY HOTEL TORONTO

Wendel's notes for his speech to the Toronto fans and media after being drafted No. 1 overall at the 1985 NHL Draft.

ABOVE: Wendel gets assistance from his Mom (right) and Harold Ballard, the Leaf's owner, in putting on a Leafs sweater on Draft Day.

in almost any situation.

In addition to Cliff and Dougie, there was another personnel move that paid off big time for the Leafs. That was the hiring of Pat Burns as coach in the summer of 1992. While Cliff and Pat have very different personalities, they complimented each other as well. They both shared a strong commitment to their convictions and were confident in their decisions. That's really important in a place like Toronto, where public scrutiny, criticism and second-guessing are a favourite past-time. And yet, it never bothered either one of them. That's why Cliff and Pat were the perfect combination for us.

And trust me; it was no artificial act or phony posturing on Pat's part. He genuinely didn't care about what people thought, said or wrote. That applied to just about everybody right across the board – the fans, the media and most of all us. His attitude was, "Boys, here's how we're going to play, no maybes, it's this way or no way."

And we all got the message.

The thing about coaches is that you don't have to love them, but you do have to respect them. I always laugh whenever I hear there's no communication between the coach and the players. That's because there never has been coach-player communication, there is only coaching. Different styles, different strategies, yeah, sure. But you're not there to be best friends and get along; the key to coaching is respect.

Pat was something else. He'd always be poking or prodding or provoking. Most of the time, it seemed he wanted, maybe even hoped, the players would hate him. It was his way of bringing the team together. He'd come in before practice and start ranting, "Okay boys, do it your way. Whatever you want, fine. Do it your way."

Because I was the captain, sometimes I'd really get both barrels. He knew that if he yelled and screamed at certain so-called "key" guys on the team that would then cause the rest of the players to rally around, say me as an example, in a show of team support. It was never intended to be personal and it never was taken that way, at least not by me. It was merely Pat's way of making us closer and tighter and stronger as a group. And so he figured by unleashing the occasional barrage in my direction it wouldn't hurt my feelings and might just help the club. His outbursts were usually planned with a specific purpose in mind, which was to push us to being a better hockey club and all of us in the dressing room understood that.

Harold Ballard welcomes Wendel to the Leafs after Toronto made the Kelvington, Sask., native their No. 1 pick in 1985.

Pat also had an almost uncanny feel for the game. You want to talk about great bench coaches, Pat was one of them. He could read the guys and he could read the game. He knew exactly the way he wanted us to play as a team, as well as the roles he wanted each of us to perform individually.

He also seemed to sense early in the game, which players were hot and which guys were struggling. And Pat would adjust accordingly. Like maybe rolling the three lines he thought were working and spotting the fourth line. Or he would move guys up or down depending on what they were doing and how well they were doing it.

Since all hockey players weren't created equal, Pat, like all great coaches, recognized individual skills and strengths, and the importance of allowing them to be utilized within an overall game plan. So that meant your role could, and likely would, change depending on whom you were on a line with. For example, when you played with Dougie on the first-line, you basically had carte blanche to do almost anything you wanted. You could be creative and take chances because it was your job to try and score.

However, as far as the other lines were concerned, the direction from Pat was loud and clear: dump and chase and keep the other team from scoring. And if you man-

MAPLE LEAF GARDENS LIMITED No. A 14484

INVOICE DATE	REFERENCE	ACCOUNT NUMBER	INVOICE AMOUNT	DEDUCTION	BALANCE
Aug.26/85	signing bonus - $100,000.00 LESS: WITHHOLDING TAX		100,000.00	40,000.00	$60,000.00

DETACH BEFORE DEPOSITING

Wendel, both humbled and excited, addresses the Toronto media for the first time at the 1985 NHL Draft.

Harold Ballard celebrates with the Leafs' top two draft choices: Wendel (left) and Ken Spangler (right).

aged to get a goal in the process, well, that would be an unexpected bonus.

Right from the very first day of training camp, there was never any doubt about how Pat expected, no demanded, that we play the game. In simple terms, his philosophy was defence first and the rest will take care of itself, provided you outwork, outhustle and outhit the opposition for 60 minutes. In Pat's system, there was no room for floaters. Even though we all knew what he wanted, it took us a few months to get it right. By January, it all came together, and sure enough, we began to win just like Pat said we would. And when we lost, it was usually close. We were always in it.

As the saying goes, we played ugly. We played close-checking, dump-and-chase hockey, which I have to admit, is pretty unspectacular hockey. But there weren't any complaints, at least not in Toronto. Funny thing, when you're winning, fans will take substance over style any time.

We were playing a very physical, in-your-face type of game, which wasn't a whole lot of fun for the other team. And leading the way a lot of nights were guys like Ozzie (Mark Osborne), Bergie (Bill Berg) and Zez (Peter Zezel). They were big, strong character guys, who were relentless and made you pay the price at both ends of the rink. Their line was also regularly assigned to shut down the other team's big guns. That means people like Mario Lemieux, Pat LaFontaine, Pierre Turgeon, Alexander Mogilny, Jeremy Roenick. Up until now in their careers, they had largely gone unnoticed, but in Pat's system they were just as pivotal to our success as the guys scoring the goals.

We finished third in the Norris Division and for the first time in two years made the playoffs. We would face Detroit in the opening round. We only finished four points behind the Red Wings in the standings, but we knew we would be tough. We were confident, but we knew they were good.

NHL
GOAL
THE NATIONAL HOCKEY LEAGUE MAGAZINE
© Professional Sports Publications
TORONTO MAPLE
WENDEL CLARK
TORONTO MAPLE LEAFS

The Leafs Hound Line: (left to right) Gary Leeman, Russ Courtnall and Wendel.

Detroit was the highest scoring team in the NHL that season, so they obviously had tremendous fire power. They also had Steve Yzerman and when things got rough, my old pal from gone-by battles, Bob Probert. Over the years, Probie and I had our share of fights and it was anticipated by everyone that at some point we would have to square off in this series, but I knew it was never going to happen.

How did I know? Because Pat Burns said so. Before the playoffs even began, he called me into his office for a private conversation, which was brief and to the point: "Clarkie, you're not fighting Probert!" And in case I didn't get it the first time, Pat repeated his message: "No matter what happens with the Red Wings, you are not under any circumstances going to fight Bob Probert."

It wasn't a request, it was an order. Pat didn't really need to elaborate or explain himself. All I knew and needed to know was that it was just one more piece of Pat's plan to give us our best chance of beating the Red Wings. And that was good enough for me.

However, it didn't take long before it looked like our bubble was going to burst. The Red Wings didn't just beat us; they destroyed us, 6-3 in Game 1 and 6-2 in Game 2.

And if losing wasn't bad enough, things got even worse for me. I didn't play very well at all, and of course, I didn't drop the gloves with Probert, which is what the world wanted and was waiting for. The media was all over me; some even questioning my courage. There were also reports floating around that a few of the Red Wings had called me "Wendy," in an attempt to taunt and goad me into responding, meaning doing something stupid. If they did, I didn't hear them.

The 1985-86 Leafs finished with a record of 25-48-7. Wendel is located on Row 2, third from left.

But it was tough to sit on the bench knowing you couldn't fight Probie to try and get something going. I can now say that seldom in my career had I felt more angry and frustrated and helpless than I did then. Angry about the back-to-back losses, frustrated about not being allowed to fight and helpless about not being able to explain why. However, I couldn't, and wouldn't, ever say a word. Just like players never go public in the playoffs about injuries, I would never go public about this Probert thing.

Sometimes the criticism is tough, but I always used to try telling people in Toronto you're probably never as good as the fans and media say you are when you're lighting things up, or as bad as they say when things are going south. You're probably somewhere in the middle. So you have to keep it all in perspective. And if they're not talking about you or writing about you, then chances are it's just about over for you. In other words, when your days of being a "story" are nearing an end, in all likelihood so too is your career.

Good publicity or bad, I've always tried to stick to a couple of basic rules in dealing with the media. First, I don't view the media as the enemy. But you can't control what's being written or said about you, so don't fight it. The media will always have the last word, which means it'll be a war you're always going to lose. So the best thing is to say nothing, or be generic, and let your play speak for itself.

And when it comes to die-hard Leaf fans, as a player, you just have to kind of resign yourself to the fact that it will always be pretty much a peaks-and-valleys situation. By that I mean, there are extremes at both ends. There tends to be over-the-top praise when things are going good and cutting, sometimes below-the-belt, criticism when they're not. And yet, the one constant, and at the end of the day what counts the most and makes our fans so special, is their passion for hockey and the Toronto Maple Leafs.

I can tell you, we were really feeling confident when we returned home to Maple Leaf Gardens for Game 3. We eked out a 4-2 win that night, but in Game 4 we were really playing our game and won a 3-2 thriller. Then we went ahead in the series with a 5-4 overtime win in Game 5 at Detroit. But to the Red Wings' credit, they bounced back and blew us out, 7-3, in Game 6 at the Gardens. That set the stage for the seventh game in the Motor City.

Although most people were convinced that going back to Detroit meant it was all over for us, we were confident that if we just continued to play "our game" in their building, we could, and would win. There was no doubt the Red Wings were the best puck-possession team in the NHL. They probably controlled 70 percent of the play in most games. But it was also true that a lot of their players, guys like Sergei Federov, always preferred making a perfect pass and wouldn't shoot the puck. So Pat's strategy was to let the Wings move the puck along the "wall" but not let them get into the danger zone, where they were absolutely lethal. The key for us was to be patient and wait for mistakes, then jump all over them and create scoring chances of our own, especially for the skill guys like Dougie and Dave Andreychuk.

We did stick to Pat's plan and we did win, upsetting the Red Wings, 4-3, in overtime. It was a really satisfying victory for all of us, but not an entirely surprising victory because we had always believed we could do it.

Naturally, we were on top of the world. But we came down to earth pretty fast because there was still plenty of highway ahead of us. The next stop was the St. Louis Blues.

Not to brag, but the way we played in that series, we should have beaten St. Louis in four or five games. Instead, it once again took us seven games. And there was only one reason why the Blues were able to push us to the limit – his name was Curtis Joseph. To say Cujo was brilliant would be an understatement. We would fire 50 or 60 shots at him almost every game. We'd just be shaking our heads. The guy was amazing. I'll tell you, if the Blues had been able to muster any kind of sustained offence, we'd have been in big, big trouble. But in the end, Cujo was hurting and worn down to the point where he had nothing left in the tank. We finally took the series in Game 7 with a 6-0 win.

There's no question that after two grueling seven-game series, we were all pretty exhausted. It would have been nice to have gotten by St. Louis in five games. But we weren't going to let fatigue be a factor. We were in the Stanley Cup semi-finals, having fun and full of confidence.

Toronto is a completely different city in the playoffs. The buzz began before the Detroit series and from there it had just kept building and building and building. There was an amazing energy and excitement in the city.

To minimize the distractions, throughout the playoffs the team stayed at the Sutton Place Hotel, not far from the rink. Before each game, we would walk to the Gardens and you could feel the electricity. It was absolutely unreal. After the game, things were even cra-

At the 1986 NHL Draft in Detroit: Wendel with his agent, Don Meehan (middle), and Joey Kocur (right).

The 1993-94 Leafs finished with a regular-season record of 43-29-12 but lost in the Western Conference finals. Wendel is located on Row 2, second from left.

zier. How crazy? We would have to wait until after midnight before we could leave the Gardens and go home or back to the hotel.

With Detroit and St. Louis now out of the way, the only obstacle remaining between us and a trip to the Stanley Cup final was Wayne Gretzky and the Los Angeles Kings, who arrived in town for the first two games at the Gardens.

I'm pretty sure what the majority of people will remember most about the series opener wasn't our 4-1 victory, but rather the "McSorley hit".

Over the years, I had my fair share of battles with Marty McSorley. We actually had a lot in common. Both of us were farm boys with brothers to scrap with; both of us were defencemen-turned-forwards, both of us played a hard-working, hard-hitting, hard-nosed style, and both of us with a reputation for standing up for ourselves and our teammates. So I had a lot of respect for Marty because he was a stand-up guy, who usually played the game the same way.

So when he absolutely demolished Dougie Gilmour at the L.A. blue line late in that game, I kind of understood the "what" and the "why." After all, the Kings were behind and being outplayed. Marty had decided to make a statement and send us a message that it was going to be a long, tough, series. Over the years, you'd better believe that when the Leafs were in need of a little boost, lots of times I had delivered that same message. I had no problem with that. But what I did have a very big problem with was how he delivered it and to which player.

Up until now, nobody had ever really run Dougie or made him a target, either during the season or the playoffs. This is exactly the way it's supposed to be. You want your scorers, your skill guys to feel comfortable and secure wheeling and dealing around the ice, not looking over their shoulders or worrying about some guy taking their head off. You want them to feel safe to do what they do. So, if a guy takes liberties with your best player you can have to answer it. Just like if anyone tried to do something to Gretzky, well, Marty would be there in a flash.

So somebody had to respond, answer the bell, and that somebody was going to be me. Pat Burns may have told me not to fight Probert, but he never said anything about McSorley. So we went at it. There was plenty of intensity and plenty of punches, which is why people

Pat Burns and the new-look 1992-93 Toronto Maple Leafs finished the regular season with a 44-29-11 record but lost in the Conference finals to the L.A. Kings.

still talk about it, I guess. Anyway, when it was over, the crowd was going wild and I was feeling pretty good, too, because I had done my job and also sent a message of my own.

And Pat wasn't going to be a problem, either. As I learned later, he had been so mad about the McSorley-Gilmour hit that he was looking to get a piece himself of L.A. coach Barry Melrose, who also happens to be a cousin of mine. Pat apparently thought Barry had ordered Marty to rough up Dougie. I really never thought that Barry would do that.

McSorley was right about one thing, the Kings weren't going to roll over and die. They won Game 2, 3-2, and then took Game 3, which was played in L.A., 4-2. We then bounced back and won the fourth game, 4-2. Back in Toronto for Game 5, we won that one by 3-2 in overtime and took a 3-2 series' lead. So now we were just one win away from a shot at the Stanley Cup when we returned to the West Coast for Game 6.

Some people say this was perhaps the greatest game I ever played as a Toronto Maple Leaf. I don't know about that, but I do know that I was hurting in a very big way. The wear and tear of the season and the playoffs had really taken a toll on me. My body felt like it was breaking down. And there was even some question about me being physically able to play at all. I had spent most of the day receiving therapy from our trainer, Chris Broadhurst. But I couldn't even finish the pre-game warm-up. After about three minutes I had to leave the ice and get more treatment. But I decided I'd give it a shot but had no idea what I would get out of my body.

It's hard to explain, but some nights you feel like you are going to be unbelievable and nothing happens, then other nights you feel like you've got nothing and you end up scoring two or three goals. And that's the way it was for me that night.

It was one of those nights when the puck just seemed to follow me. I just couldn't do anything wrong. I actually ended up with a hat trick and I remember the third goal best. We were down, 4-3, and had pulled our goalie, Felix Potvin, for an extra attacker, which was me. I came through the high slot when Dougie turned with the puck in the corner. All the L.A. defenders were covering everybody except me and Dougie hit me with a perfect pass. The puck lay nice and flat on the ice, just the way you want it, and I just ripped a wrist-shot into the net, tying

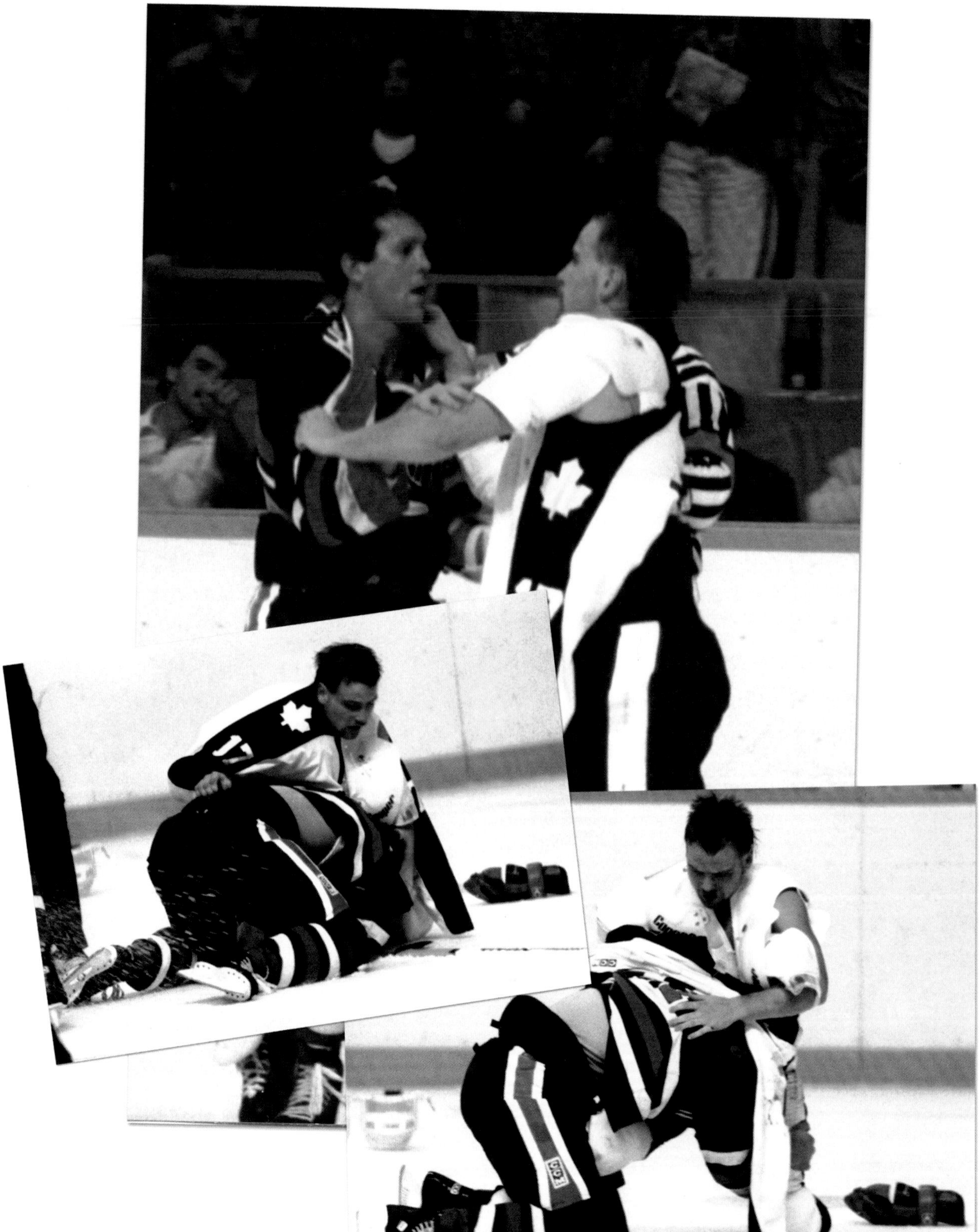

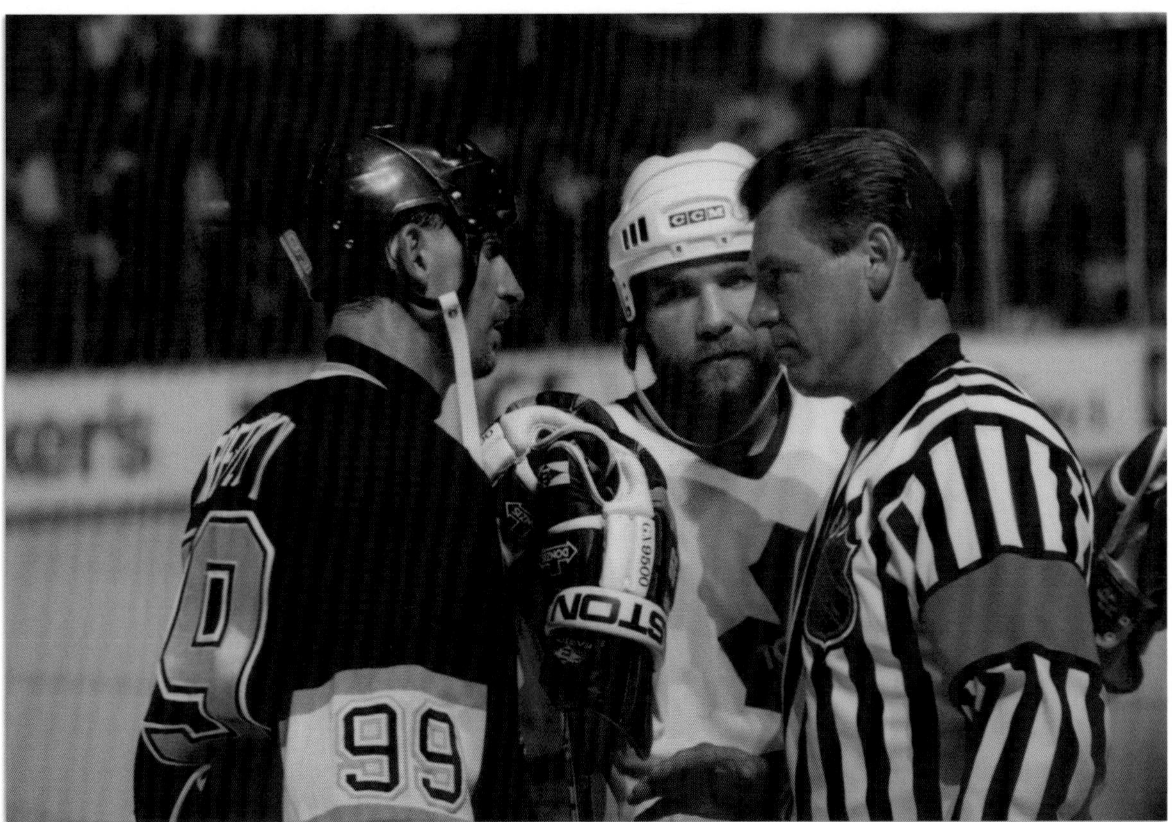

OPPOSITE PAGE: OPPOSITE PAGE: Wendel brawls with Edmonton's Craig MacTavish. **ABOVE:** Wayne Gretzky (99) and Wendel huddle with referee Dan Marouelli to discuss a problem on the ice during the 1993 NHL playoffs.

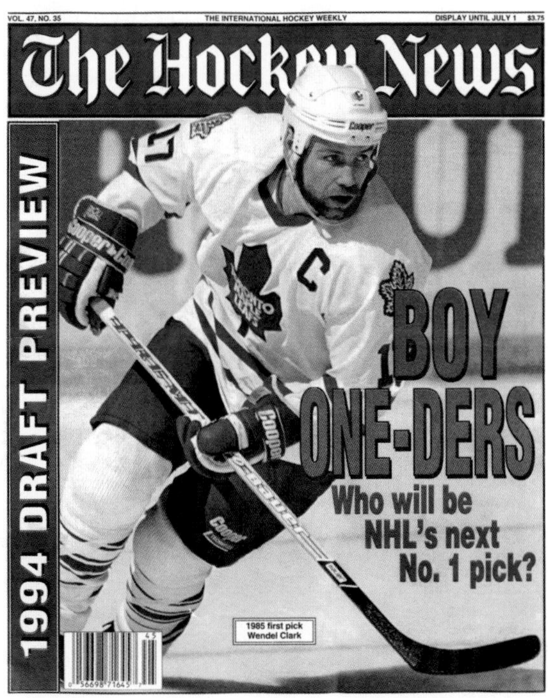

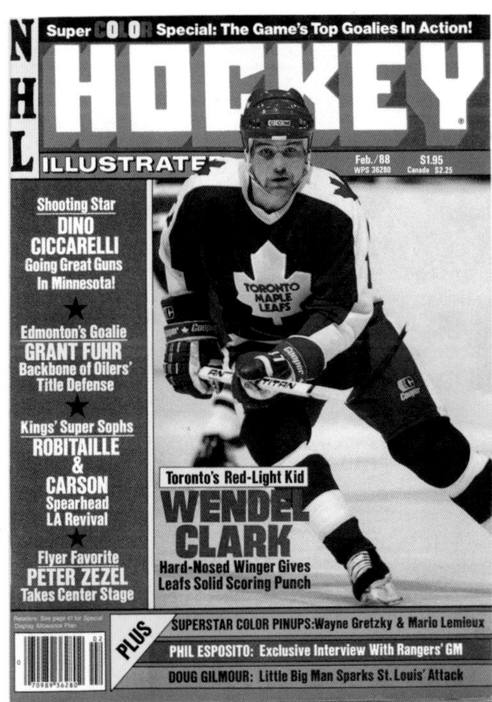

Wendel gets a hug from his cousin and LA Kings coach, Barry Melrose, on the ice during the 1993 NHL playoffs.

Up until now, the "Great One" had not had a great playoff, at least, not by his standards. And it was a story the Toronto media wouldn't let go of, some even suggesting that maybe he didn't have it any more. Well, let me tell you, that kind of talk was the last thing we wanted to hear said about Gretzky. You don't wake up a sleeping bear, especially when that bear just might be the best hockey player who ever lived.

Something I've noticed over the years is that players like Gretzky, the "special ones," are not only blessed with amazing skills, but they also possess a certain unique "presence." And that presence, along with their "legend status," under the right circumstances, can be almost as important and influential, as their talents. For example, look at what happened in overtime of Game 6.

Leaf fans will never forget what happened and neither will I. Simply put, Gretz high-sticked Dougie and got away with it. Everybody saw it, except referee Kerry Fraser. Dougie was even bleeding from the chin, but still no penalty. Since I was the captain, it was my responsibility to confront Kerry about the call, or in this instance, the "non call." But you know you're never going to win. Referees do not change their minds.

We were obviously upset about that non call and the boarding penalty he gave Glenn Anderson in the final seconds of regulation. We couldn't believe there was a penalty called on that play, that late in the game.

And then, to add more salt to the wound, none other than Gretz scores the winning goal, forcing Game 7.

We were disappointed, but certainly not down.

the game and forcing overtime.

I prided myself on the wrist shot. You don't see them as much any more. Alex Ovechkin is bringing it back a little. But my Dad wouldn't let me slap the puck as a kid, so while playing defence I had to shoot the puck from the blue line and score with the wrist shot.

Anyway, all of us felt confident we were going to win the game and go to the Stanley Cup. But I guess what we all forgot about, was the "Gretzky factor."

Another Game 7 was no big deal. We had been there twice before already and won them both. Not only that, but we would be back home at the Gardens.

Remember in Game 6 in L.A., when I could do no wrong? Well, that's what Game 7 was like for Gretzky. He did everything right. I mean, the guy was pure magic. He was involved in all of the L.A goals, including the winner, which he scored himself by bouncing the puck off defenceman Dave Ellett's skate for a 5-4 victory. Later, Gretz said it was the best game he'd ever played.

Whether it was or wasn't, all I know is that he and the Kings were headed to Montreal for the Stanley Cup Final.

What made that loss even harder to take, was the fact that deep down we believed we would have beaten the Montreal Canadiens. And can you just imagine the impact of a Toronto-Montreal Stanley Cup final on this country. Canada would probably have closed down for a couple of weeks.

Of course, we never did find out.

One other thing I do know for certain is that the Canadiens definitely did not want to play us. One of their stars, Kirk Muller, told me so. They knew we'd be so pumped mentally and so tough physically that they'd really have their hands full – maybe too full. As it turned out, Montreal did beat the Kings to win the Stanley Cup.

For us, it was a long summer. To be so close and then ultimately fall short, in an odd sort of way, I'm not sure if the guys, as a group, ever fully recovered.

When the 1993-94 season rolled around, we got off to a tremendous start, winning 10 straight, but then we cooled off considerably, winning about half our games the rest of the way and there was just a different feeling.

In the '94 playoffs, we beat Chicago and played well, then we had a really tough series with San Jose before once again advancing to the Stanley Cup semi-finals, this time against the Vancouver Canucks. Vancouver was a big, strong club, who played a tough, physical and hard-hitting brand of hockey. We won the first game of the series, but they won the next four.

When it was over, it didn't feel like we were as close as we were in '93, but you still had the overall feeling as a team that we were close and, as for reaching our Stanley Cup dream, maybe next year.

THE TORONTO STAR

SPORTS

Saturday, July 2, 1994 Section C

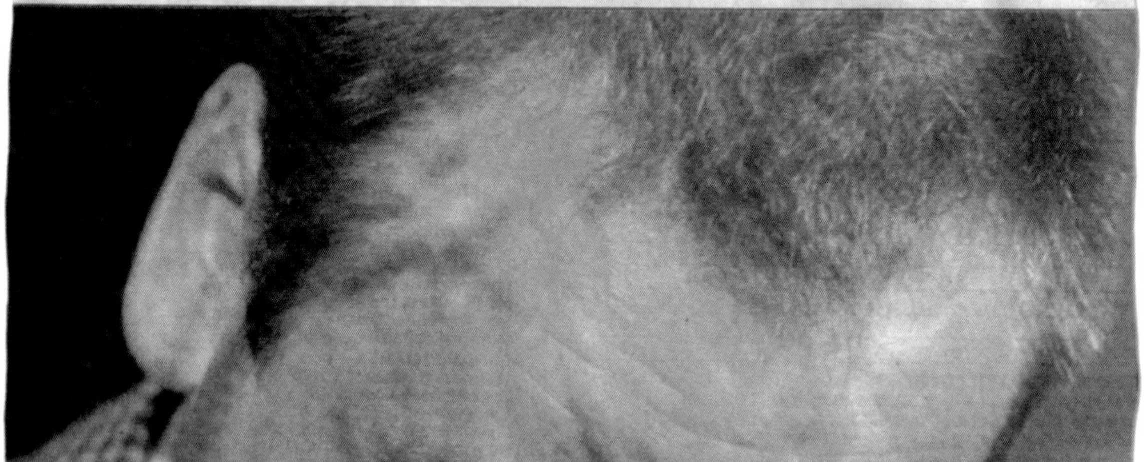

ANDREW STAWICKI / TORONTO STA

BIDDING ADIEU: Wendel Clark wiped away tears at farewell press conference yesterday, but maintained his sense of humor. When asked if he spoke French, Clark replied: "My French teacher in Grade 7 told me I was going to have know this some day, I should have stuck with it." Story on page C4.

Say it ain't so!

By SCOTT BURNSIDE
Toronto Sun

■ *Leafs trade captain Wendel Clark to Quebec Nordiques*

Farewell! Wendel, *adieu*! We hardly knew you!

A tough-as-nails team leader and one of the most popular athletes in the city, Wendel Clark is gone.

The shocking news that Clark was headed to Quebec City's Nordiques after a blockbuster draft-day trade raced like a firestorm through the city.

"I'm in shock! Wendel's part of this city," moaned Steve Greenaway, 28, a chef at Gert's on Front St. "I'm at a loss."

"That's crazy! I like Wendel Clark," said a stunned Bob Hesse, 45, when he learned of the deal. "They'll be lynching somebody tomorrow!"

"There'll be hell to pay," added a security guard listening in on the details at the Commerce Court West building downtown.

Even provincial Tory Leader Mike Harris, was miffed.

"We're not happy about this," Harris said before speaking at a rally at the St. Lawrence Market. "He's a large part of the hope and the drive on this team."

Never one to stray far from his political roots, Harris did see one bright spot about Clark moving to Quebec. "Maybe it'll be good for national unity."

CLARK
He's gone

Clark, 27, was the Leafs' first pick in the 1985 draft. A native of Kelvington, Sask., Clark was the archetypical Canadian hockey player and local fans embraced him for that.

And despite sometimes inconsistent play and a series of nagging injuries, a special bond was forged between player and fans.

"Everybody knows Wendel Clark," Maple Leaf cab driver Lou Grossman, 66, said. "You know, sock'em, bash 'em hockey."

The Leafs also gave up dependable defenceman Sylvain Lefebvre and promising minor-leaguer Landon Wilson.

In return, the Nordiques sent Mats Sundin, a big, talented centre with a questionable work ethic. Olympian Todd Warriner and veteran defenceman Garth Butcher will also don Leafs jerseys.

"It'll help the Leafs because they got the best player in the deal (Sundin)," Ken Combden, 17, said.

Tantalized by thoughts of a possible Stanley Cup the past two years, the question Leafs fans wait to have answered is whether the deal might possibly yield a championship. If the answer turns out to be yes ... Wendel? Wendel who?

MORE
■ *Wendel heads east. Roundup on* Pages 106-108

The Long Road
Back to Toronto

Losing to Vancouver in the 1994 Stanley Cup semi-final was a real blow to the entire Leafs organization, the players and management alike. And it was different than the disappointment we had felt the year before when we lost to L.A. It's hard to explain, but I felt we were much closer to winning the Stanley Cup after losing to the Kings than after we lost to the Canucks. I still believed we were a very good hockey team, but I wasn't sure if we were good enough to win the Cup.

There was a lot of talk in the media about various moves the Leafs would be making in the off-season. Adding fuel to the fire was the fact that management had also said publically that we were still a couple of players away from getting to the next level. So I think everybody expected some changes were on the way.

That summer was probably the first time I didn't pay much attention to all of the trade speculation and my name never was really mentioned. I'd been injured a lot early in my career, so there wasn't much trade talk then and now, stats-wise, I was coming off my best season in the NHL – 46 goals and 30 assists in just 64 games. So I was feeling pretty sure I had nothing to worry about. I had no reason to think that anything might be going on involving me in any deals the Leafs were working on. Maybe I should have remembered that if Wayne Gretzky can be traded, so can anybody. Including me.

And then came the bombshell. It was on Tuesday, June 28th, the day of the 1994 NHL Entry Draft in Hartford. It would be the day I was no longer a Toronto Maple Leaf. And like most really important events in people's lives, I can remember exactly where I was and exactly what I was doing when I found out about the trade.

I had spent that day shooting a Cheerios cereal TV commercial in Mississauga, west of Toronto. That evening, as I was driving back toward downtown Toronto, I stopped at an ESSO station near Bathurst Street and Lakeshore, right across from the old Molson brewery. As I was putting gas into the car, I remembered it was draft day, so I turned on the radio to find out who our first round selection was (goalie Eric Fichaud) and if anything else interesting had gone on that day (back then I didn't have a cell phone). So there I was, pumping

Au revoir, Wendel!

Leafs captain goes to Quebec in huge trade

By Damien Cox
Sports Reporter

HARTFORD — The Maple Leafs are a more skilled hockey club today, but they've lost some of their soul.

In a dramatic, blockbuster trade on the floor of the National Hockey League draft yesterday, the Maple Leafs dealt captain Wendel Clark to the Quebec Nordiques, ending the 27-year-old Clark's nine-year run as one of the most popular players ever to wear the Toronto blue-and-white.

"I'm going to a different team to play hockey — it's not the end of the world," Clark said last night after hearing about the trade on the radio.

"Bonjour," he said with a laugh when asked if he could speak French. "Hockey is bilingual. You don't have to be able to speak French."

Six-player deal, C1

Maple Leaf head coach Pat Burns said he was shocked by the news, "like everyone else . . . But you've got to give up gold to get gold."

The precious gem the Leafs received in return for their rough-and-ready leader was Swedish centre Mats Sundin, a 23-year-old rated by most as one of the most skilled young players in hockey.

The Leafs also received veteran defenceman Garth Butcher and young forward Todd Warriner in the deal, and included defenceman Sylvain Lefebvre and prospect Landon Wilson in the package sent to the Nordiques.

The Leafs and Nords also swapped first-round picks, and Leaf general manager Cliff Fletcher had hoped to land Brett Lindros, brother of Philadelphia star Eric Lindros, with the pick. But the New York Islanders grabbed the younger Lindros first.

Clark, the Leafs' captain since 1991, is coming off a career year in which he scored 46 goals and was selected to play in the NHL all-star game.

"This was a very emotional decision to make on our part," said Fletcher. "We agonized over it for weeks and weeks."

Clark, who spoke to reporters outside his Madison Ave. home last night, was gracious about the news.

"I have no hard feelings towards anyone," he told The Star's Paul Hunter.

BERNARD WEIL / TORONTO STAR

SAYING SO LONG: Leaf captain Wendel Clark gives a wink and a wave as he leaves his Toronto home last night after learning of his trade to Quebec.

Wendel waives good-bye to the Toronto fans after being traded to the Quebec Nordiques in 1994.

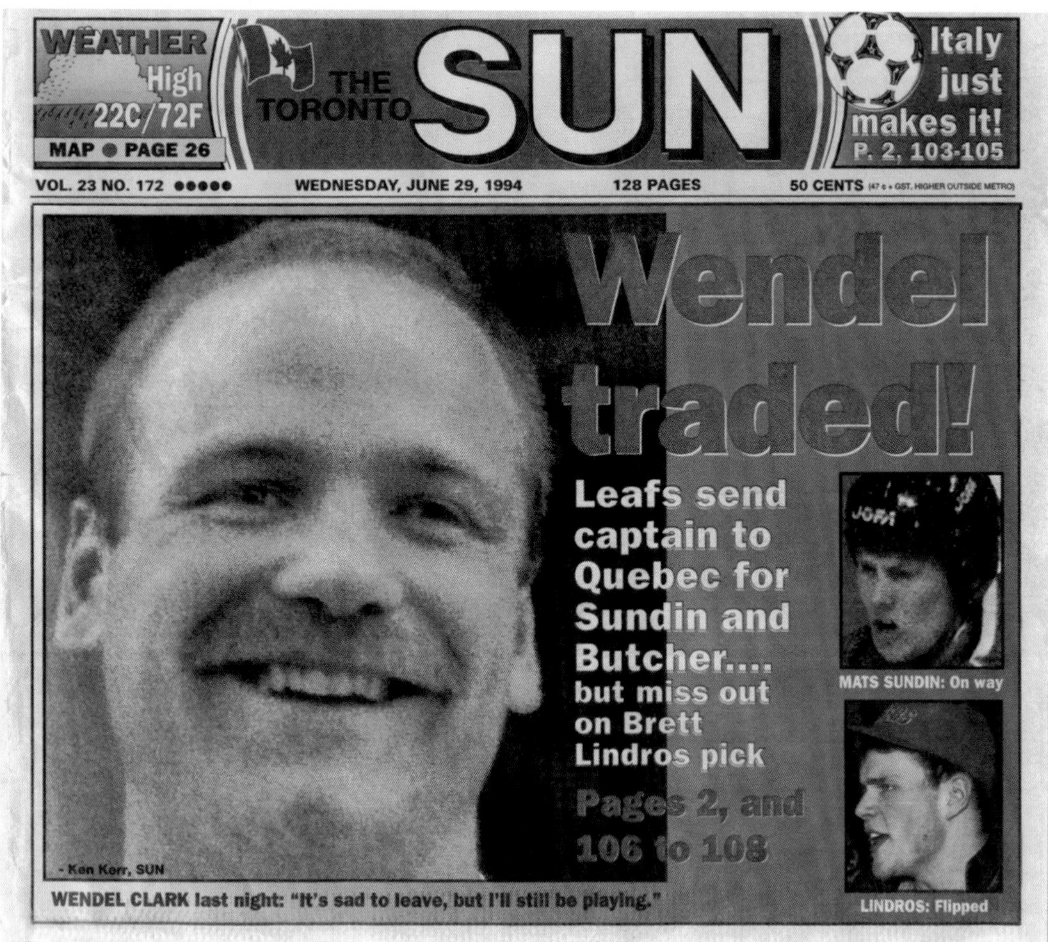
WËATHER High 22C/72F MAP ● PAGE 26

THE TORONTO SUN

Italy just makes it! P. 2, 103-105

VOL. 23 NO. 172 ●●●●● WEDNESDAY, JUNE 29, 1994 128 PAGES 50 CENTS

Wendel traded!

Leafs send captain to Quebec for Sundin and Butcher.... but miss out on Brett Lindros pick

Pages 2, and 106 to 108

- Ken Kerr, SUN

WENDEL CLARK last night: "It's sad to leave, but I'll still be playing."

MATS SUNDIN: On way

LINDROS: Flipped

The Leafs' trade of their captain sent shock waves to the Toronto fans and media.

gas when I first heard the news: I had been traded to the Quebec Nordiques.

It was a multi-player deal: Sylvain Lefebvre, Landon Wilson and I, along with a first-round draft choice, to Quebec for Mats Sundin, Garth Butcher, Todd Warriner and the Nordiques' first-round pick.

Funny, but my first reaction was not anger or disbelief. It was simply, "Oh well, I guess I'm no longer a Toronto Maple Leaf." Then I thought, "Wow, how did they keep a six-player, block-buster deal like that so quiet and for so long?" I mean a trade this big had to be in the works for a while and there wasn't even a whisper.

A couple of minutes later, the full shock of what happened finally hit me and I can tell you, it felt about as hard as any check or punch I'd ever taken.

There was tremendous disappointment and disbelief.

As I mentioned, my ninth season with the Leafs had been my best and after going to the Stanley Cup semifinals two years straight, the team was headed in the right direction. All we needed was a little fine tuning to take a real run at the Cup, but I didn't think I would be part of the fine tuning.

I then thought about all the years of persevering through the losing, the injuries and the turmoil; playing hurt and sacrificing my body and doing whatever was necessary for the sake of the team. Now, just when we were almost where we needed to be to go all the way, they send me packing and the dream is over. Honestly, for the first time I think I aged a little bit that day. I also grew up a lot. I realized for the first time, playing hockey is a job and hockey is a business.

It's not really my nature to get mad, or overly upset about anything. I usually try to take things in stride and move on. So I wasn't really angry, but I did try to rationalize why Cliff Fletcher had made the deal.

Everybody knew that Cliff had been trying to add a

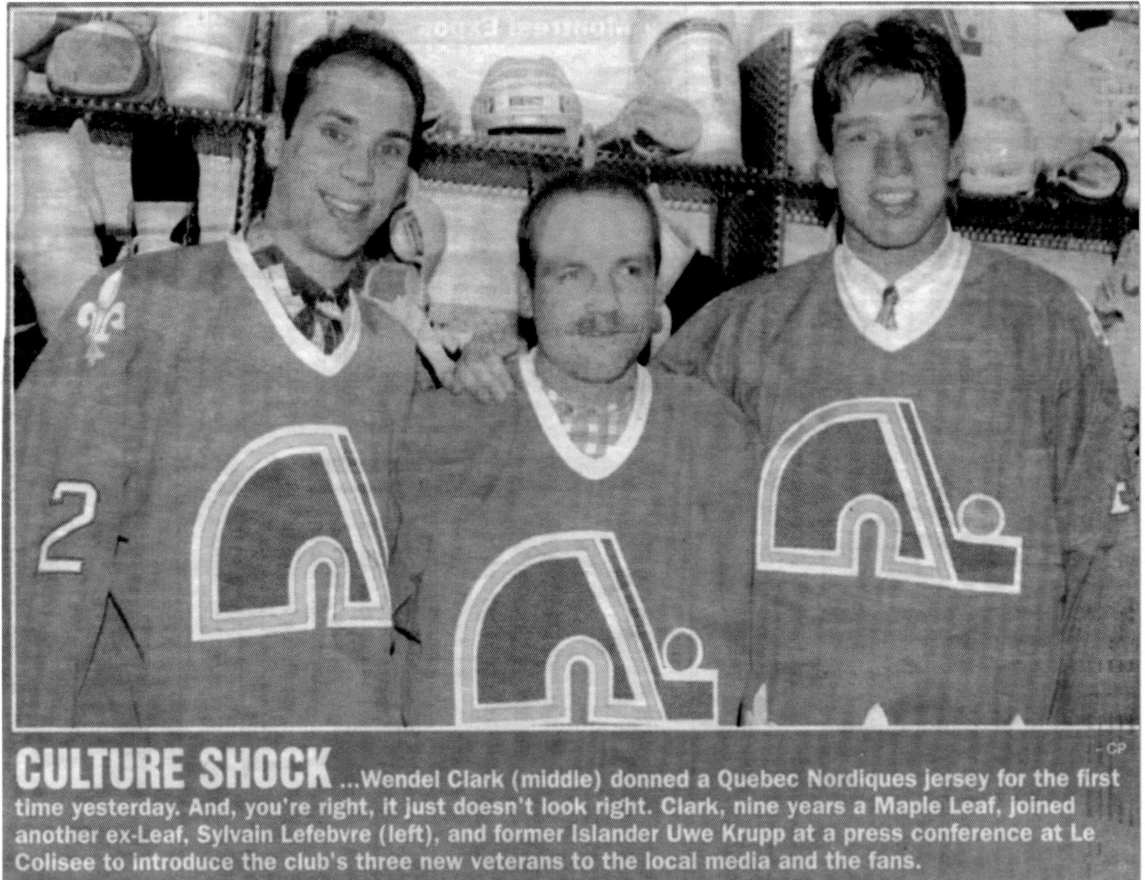

Wendel and former Leaf teammate, Sylvain Lefebvre (left), pose with Uwe Krupp (right) after their arrival in Quebec in 1994.

player or two, who would help us get to the next level. And there was no question that Mats Sundin was one of the most talented young players in the NHL. He was also a good guy, so nobody would have to worry about him being disruptive or a distraction. But one thing you do have to worry about when you make a trade is the effect it will have on the team; how the new players will change the team chemistry, and whether it will be for the better or not. This is something no GM can ever predict. And Mats and I were very different players and people. He was also a lot different than Dougie Gilmour, who Cliff eventually wanted Mats to replace as the team leader in the dressing room and on the ice. But until that happened, the Leafs would still be Dougie's team.

So for me, that summer was mostly about good-byes to friends and fans. The fans were truly something else. They even staged a huge event in my honour in North York. I was really going to miss them and Toronto. It had really been an amazing ride.

It was no secret that Quebec City was not exactly a favourite destination for NHL players. Most fans will remember Eric Lindros' refusal to report to the Nordiques in 1991 after they'd had made him their No. 1 draft choice. But there was no way I was going to buck the system. I accepted the trade as being part of the business. Not only that, and this may sound pretty simple, but I'd always felt extremely fortunate just to be playing in the NHL.

Because of the lockout, the 1994-95 season did not start until January. Once we got to training camp, it didn't take long to realize the Nordiques had a very strong group of great young hockey talent, with guys like Joe Sakic, Peter Forsberg and Mike Ricci. At the time, I was only 28 but I was one of the "old men" on the team.

It was also pretty obvious that the Nordiques were a much closer team than most. The main reason was the language barrier. Quebec, of course, is a French-speaking city, and the majority of our guys spoke English only. So we spent a lot more time hanging out together than a lot of teams, which created an amazing team spirit.

There was never a language problem in stores or restaurants. However, when it came to dealing with reporters after practices or games, since the questions would be in French, a lot of times we didn't actually have a clue what they were asking us. So our French-speaking teammates became our translators. I think that experience helped me to understand what some of the European players go through when they first come to the NHL.

Speaking of the Quebec media, if you think you're under the microscope in Toronto, which you are, the scrutiny you get as a Nordique is also pretty intense. You can't go anywhere or do anything without the press finding out.

For example, my brother, Kerry, came to visit me and catch a couple of games during our playoff series with the New York Rangers that spring. Kerry's a little bigger and taller than me, but there is a family resemblance. And being a young single guy, he was pretty impressed with Quebec City's night life. So while I'd be at home getting my rest for the Rangers, Kerry would be out on the town enjoying himself. I mean, he must have been really enjoying himself because a day or two later, there's a big story in the newspaper that said I was spotted out partying all night, instead of focusing on the Rangers.

I really got roasted by the press. It seems at one of the clubs, somebody mistook Kerry for me. He thought it was funny, but I took all the lumps.

The following season (1995-96), Quebec moved and so did I, but not to the same place. That summer when the Nordiques re-located to Denver and became the Avalanche, they promised to re-negotiate my contract. For the first time in my career, I had some negotiating power. But the contract talks weren't happening and I wasn't happy about it. So I stayed in Kelvington, deciding not to report to training camp until a deal was done.

And then, with the season just starting, the Avalanche made a three-team, three-player trade. I went to the New York Islanders, Claude Lemieux went west to Colorado and my old buddy, Steve Thomas, was off to play for the New Jersey Devils.

What bothered me the most about leaving the Nordiques/Avalanche, is that I knew they were so close

JIM PROUDFOOT

Clark leads Nords by both word and deed

QUEBEC CITY

CHRIS SIMON was on his feet at the Quebec Nordiques' bench during a recent match, arguing with coach Marc Crawford — screaming at him, actually.

Wendel Clark leaned over and bluntly instructed Simon to sit down and shut up.

Protest was mild and brief. This had become a given around the National Hockey League during Clark's three years as captain of the Maple Leafs; he speaks with authority and is ignored at one's peril.

In the dressing room afterward, Clark explained that embarrassing the coach in public was strictly a no-no. Disagreements can arise, of course. But they're to be dealt with internally.

"Emotions go up during a game. Sometimes people get carried away but there are things you can do, as a veteran," says Clark, whose transfer here was one of last year's unhappiest events in Toronto sport.

"You can head off situations you see building. Like Crow (Crawford) wants a positive bench. So you try to help people who've missed the point.

Leafs can't overcome the loss of Wendel Clark

TORONTO STAR FILE PHOTO BY DOUG GRIFFIN

BIG FACTOR: A back injury has kept Wendel Clark under wraps all season and there's no telling when he'll be back in Leaf lineup. With Clark, Leafs improved by 13 points in 1986-87 and won opening round in playoffs and led a second series before losing to Detroit.

JIM PROUDFOOT

You'll find no defence of the Maple Leafs' management in this space. These guys, as the saying goes, would mishandle a two-car funeral.

But hey, this is Christmastime. Yuletide and all that. Kindness and generosity are supposed to prevail. So let's break down, quit abusing the helpless and say something the least bit positive about this benighted organization.

The Leafs have been dreadfully unlucky where Wendel Clark is concerned.

They finally got it right at the 1985 National Hockey League draft and in Clark, obtained that one extraordinary player around whom they could develop a contender.

And now he's of no use to them. What's worse, there's no indication when his chronic back miseries are apt to clear up — or, indeed, whether they ever will.

Clark was able to take part in 28 games last season — three here, a few there and finally 17 when he decided he'd try to carry on despite continuous pain. He gave up early in February and hasn't appeared since, although he skates forlornly through each practice and toils faithfully in the exercise room.

Fell to pieces

Basically, though, his condition defies accurate diagnosis and therefore, no timetable for recovery is available. Like so many fellow backache sufferers, he lives on hope.

Now maybe you've forgotten what happened when Clark was at his bombastic best, in his second NHL campaign. The Leafs added 13 points to the output of the previous year, won their opening round in the Stanley Cup tournament and led a second series before losing to Detroit.

At that time, you could see something beginning to take shape. With added experience, Clark would be made captain and the Leafs could start to build on those modest 1987 successes. But then Clark got hurt and before long, the whole thing was falling to pieces.

The Detroit Red Wings, Pittsburgh Penguins and New Jersey Devils are three outfits which once were Toronto's neighbors in the slums of the NHL.

Thanks to outstanding draft picks (Steve Yzerman, Mario Lemieux and Sean Burke, respectively), they've risen to respectability and beyond. These are exceptional players, see, but their importance is subtler than that. They cause their colleagues to improve around them and that's what Clark was able to do for the Leafs. The Gardens athletes the fans now revile would have been better on account of Clark's leadership. And now? Who knows? Kids like these are awfully hard to find. The Leafs may have used up their quota for this decade.

In short: Mort Greenberg's 35th Christmas card campaign totalled almost $12,500 for local charities, highlighted by $4,821.35 to the Sportsmen's Corner of The Star Santa Claus Fund. Greenberg is a veteran newsreel cameraman, specializing in sports, and uses his extensive contacts during four weeks of canvassing each December. You get one of the cards Greenberg designs for himself, then you make a donation. He also gave $4,328 to The Sun's Variety Village project, $3,000 to the Special Olympics and $300 to the Canadian Children's Foundation . . . A $100 gift to the Corner was in memory of **Punch Imlach** and a time when Maple Leaf Gardens really stood for something in hockey . . . **John** and **Mary Ann Newediuk** contributed $100 each . . . A $25 submission was from the organizers of the Excalibur Volleyball Classic, to be held at York Jan. 6 to 8. They announce that Long Beach State will be on hand, from California, along with the defending champions from Penn State.

Leo Cahill dropped by with his $30 cheque. The former general manager of the Argos said he was still contemplating his next move and wondering whether he really wants to remain in football . . . As the Edmonton Eskimos' offensive coach, **Steve Goldman** had a lot to do with **Damon Allen's** development as a quarterback. Allen is becoming a free agent now and Goldman is the new head coach in Ottawa. Make of that what you will . . . The Compuware outfit in Detroit wants to sell the Windsor Spitfires and put a new Ontario Hockey League franchise in Cobo Hall, right beside the Red Wings' home at Joe Louis Arena . . . The Boston Bruins might trade goaltender **Reggie Lemelin** because of the way young **Mike Jeffrey** is playing in the minors . . . Former Toronto captain **Rick Vaive,** now with the Blackhawks, is available.

to being a championship team. About the only thing missing was a proven goaltender and they solved that problem in a very big way, getting Patrick Roy after his dispute with Montreal. Roy gave the Avalanche everything they needed. Of course, just like I figured they would, that spring the Avalanche won the Stanley Cup. So once again, I had been close but there would be no cigar, just like it had been in Toronto.

Life can be like that, I guess.

Even though I was having a pretty good year with the Islanders, there were rumours making the rounds that I was on the trading block. I didn't pay all that much attention. We hear those things all the time. But with only about a month or so left in the regular season, sure enough it happened. Not only was I being traded, but I was being traded to the Toronto Maple Leafs, along with Mathieu Schneider and a prospect, D.J. Smith. In return, the Islanders would get Darby Hendrickson, Kenny Jonsson, a youngster named Sean Haggerty, plus a first-round draft choice (who turned out to be Roberto Luongo).

I was surprised about being traded, but I was really happy and excited about going back to Toronto, which seemed like home. But in the two seasons I was away, it was a much different team than the one I'd left. A lot of the guys whom I had played with were now gone. It was a team in transition – and it was changing from being "Dougie's team" to "Mats' team." But still, it was great to be back home with all my friends and familiar surroundings and, of course, the fans.

I stayed with the Leafs for two more seasons, but I knew I wouldn't be returning for the 1998-99 season. That summer (1998) I was a free-agent and signed with the Tampa Bay Lightning. They wanted me primarily to be a mentor, or role-model, for their young star, Vinny Lecavalier. Things went really well in Tampa. In addition to working with Vinny, I was also having a real good season, offensively. I was chosen to play in my last All-Star game that season, which was pretty cool and pretty special.

Then, at the trading deadline, I was once again on the move, this time to the Detroit Red Wings. They had won two consecutive Stanley Cups in 1997 and 1998 and Detroit had a new nickname: "Hockeytown." Playing on a team like the Red Wings with a great player like Steve Yzerman and for a coaching genius like Scotty Bowman,

Shortly after the 1999 NHL All-Star Game, Wendel was traded to the defending NHL champion Detroit Red Wings. He wore sweater Number "71".

both Hall of Famers, would have been perfect except for one thing. We were upset by Colorado in the playoffs, so there wasn't going to be a third straight Cup for the Wings, or a first Stanley Cup for me. Which, once again, was very disappointing.

That summer I signed with Chicago for the 1999-2000 season. Dougie was also playing for the Blackhawks. Most of the time in Chicago, I was hurt and played in only 13 games. In January, I signed with the Leafs, making my third and final trip back to play in Toronto.

It's funny how things work out sometimes. For the first nine years of my career, I had only played with the Leafs. (To be with the same team for that long is fairly unusual in the NHL.) But in the next six years, I played with five different teams, plus two different return stints with the Leafs. Needless to say, my bags were always packed.

Toronto had a good team, but this time round, my job was to play more of a support role rather than rekindle what once was. This was just fine with me. As always, I was happy to be home.

We beat Ottawa in the opening round of the playoffs and then took on New Jersey in the next series. Once again, I got hurt, and once again it was my back. I couldn't dress for Game 6 against the Devils, which we wound up losing, 3-0. And then it was over.

By early summer, I still hadn't made a final decision on my future. Some teams talked to me about a contract, but there was nothing serious. There was no question that I was now at a crossroads in my career. So I sat down with Donnie Meehan. Not only had he always been my agent, but he was also a close and trusted friend. Donnie realized that my career was coming to an end. His only advice was, "Wendel, don't linger, don't wait ... make sure it's your choice and not a choice somebody else makes for you."

At that stage of my career, I was really paying the price for my style of play over the past 15 seasons. I was 32, but my body felt like 52. Timing-wise, the chance to get back to Toronto and play a little in the playoffs again, it had been great.

That, combined with the fact that I'd always planned on coming back and spending the next stage of my life with my family in Toronto, well, in my head and my heart, I knew it was the time to retire.

But even when you know it's the right decision, retirement is never easy. Leaving the game is tough. I mean, you've spent basically your whole life around a hockey rink. Hockey is the only thing you really know.

When you're playing, you spend so much of your time and energy focused on some aspect of the game. It's even worse when you're injured, because you're always rehabbing at the rink trying to get healthy again so you can get back into the lineup.

As much as people tell you not to worry about it and that you will have lots of good ideas that you can now follow up on in retirement, you're never really as sure about it as they are.

Like I said, the only thing I really knew a lot about was hockey. So calling it quits can be a little scary.

I officially announced my retirement on June 29, 2000.

Afterword, I knew exactly what my "first-year, exit-from-the-game project" would be. I was going to build a new house for my family on the property I'd bought in

Tampa Bay Lightning, 1998-99

New York Islanders, 1995-96

Chicago Blackhawks, 1999-2000

VOL. 47, NO. 40 THE INTERNATIONAL HOCKEY WEEKLY SEPT. 2, 1994 $2.95

The Hockey News

BOB PROBERT
Hawks standing by troubled tough guy

Wendel Clark
Quebec Nordiques

LABOR PAINS
Owners, players at loggerheads

SKATE GUIDE
Stride into season with special section

CALLING THE SHOTS
THN cues up '94-95 season

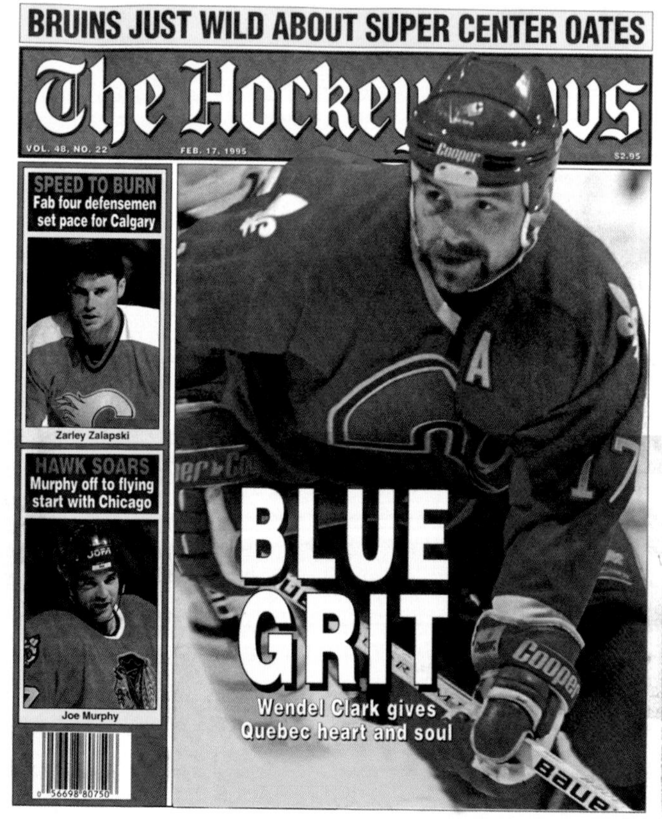

BRUINS JUST WILD ABOUT SUPER CENTER OATES

The Hockey News

VOL. 48, NO. 22 FEB. 17, 1995 $2.95

SPEED TO BURN
Fab four defensemen set pace for Calgary

Zarley Zalapski

HAWK SOARS
Murphy off to flying start with Chicago

Joe Murphy

BLUE GRIT
Wendel Clark gives Quebec heart and soul

ABOVE: Wendel played in his last NHL All-Star Game in 1999, which was held in St. Petersburg, Fla.
BELOW: During a break in the action at the 1999 All-Stars Skills Contest, Wendel (17) enjoys a chat with Colorado's Peter Forsberg (21).

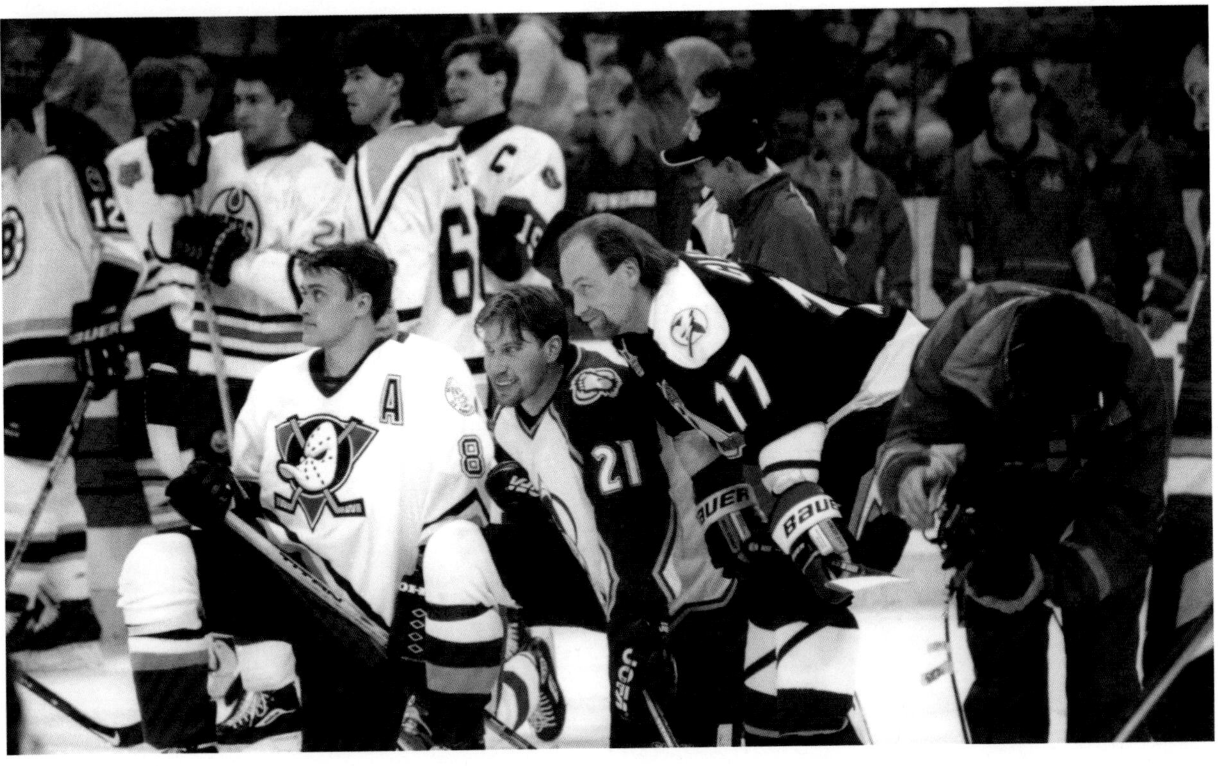

Clark's home in style

TONY BOCK / TORONTO STAR

Wendel Clark celebrates his first goal in the first period of his first game as a reborn Leaf at Maple Leaf Gardens last night. Leafs beat Dallas 3-0. Story, E1.

Saturday, March 16, 1996 Section E

King City, which is north of Toronto.

Just about every day for the next 12 months, that's what I did. It kept me busy and gave me a different daily routine. So I didn't have time to worry about trying to figure out the future.

In life, at least in my life, I knew it was really important that I continue to have a regimen, because that's what hockey is all about. A regular routine is what an NHL player is used to and needs. Of course, as much as the family home is home, the rink is also your home – it's the rock in your life. It's where you work and where you feel safe. It's where you hang out and drink coffee and tell bad stories and even worse jokes. It's where, regardless of where you happen to come from, you're never a stranger or an outsider, because everybody has something in common. That's the bond of being a hockey player on the same team with the same goals. And that's why guys like Wayne Gretzky and Mario Lemieux and Steve Yzerman stay in the game.

One of the things I've missed the most is the rush of the game. The biggest rush is when you're in the playoffs, which is what Kevin Lowe said I would miss more than anything else. The crowd is louder and the atmosphere is more exciting and the game is more important than it is during the regular season. The playoffs are also the most fun, so Kevin was right.

I never wanted to retire feeling negative about the game or how I played it. Professional athletes are naturally about the most competitive people you'll find anywhere. Tell them they can't do something and their immediate reaction is to prove you wrong. The worst thing you can do, though, is try to prove them wrong when you're too old.

I've always hated watching a great player become average.

I never wanted to be that player.

Once a Leaf . . .
ALWAYS A LEAF

❑ The pride of Kelvington ponders life after hockey

By P. J. Kennedy
For The StarPhoenix

Wendel Clark is thankful for every year he spent in the National Hockey League — especially the 12 seasons he played after doctors said he should quit.

Clark, who often fought to recover from painful back injuries, was told early on he should retire.

"There were doctors who said that I should quit in that third year. I played 15. I was supposed to quit after three, so there's a bonus of 12," says Clark, 34, who finally retired last June.

"Nobody's ever 100 per cent, even if you never played hockey. Whether you're a farmer or work in an office, if you've got a sore back, you learn how to deal with it," says Clark, a native of Kelvington.

—CP File Photo

A tearful Wendel Clark announces his retirement from hockey in Toronto last June

His career — of which he spent 12½ seasons with the Leafs — spanned 793 regular season games and 95 playoff contests. He scored 367 goals, added another 256 assists and a hard-hitting 1,891 penalty minutes.

Today, he is now learning how to deal with life off the ice, but not away from the game.

The immensely popular Clark, who first broke into the league with the Leafs in 1985-86, is enjoying the transition from stellar athlete to family man.

Many mornings are spent overseeing construction of a new home for him, his wife, and their three children on 40 acres north of Toronto.

But he's still a Leaf on game days.

That's when he steps up as community representative for Maple Leaf Sports and Entertainment.

"Wendel's a Leaf for life," says Tom Anselmi, who's responsible for marketing, sales, corporate partnerships, and broadcasting for the Leafs and NBA Raptors.

What Clark is asked to do, Anselmi says, is be a part of the organization "to excite our fans, to inspire our employees, and to bring pride to our community.

"When you have a guy like Wendel who shares those values, you put those values to work for you."

General manager Ken Dryden adds it's only natural Clark should have some ongoing association with the team. "Wendel is a Leaf, and he's a great Leaf and that's how people see him. (He) is immensely likable. He's a good guy. People can detect who is real and who is authentic and who isn't. Wendel's a real person."

And Clark says his new job is a perfect fit because it allows him to remain affiliated with the club. He hosts groups at Air Canada Centre, visits corporate and charity suites before and during games, and goes out into the community to promote the Leafs and Raptors at various events.

He hasn't skated since he retired, but he attends numerous charity events and he's finding that he's a lot more comfortable now in a public speaking role.

Retirement for any professional athlete is a major change, says Dryden. "It's a hard step to stop and move to the next. What you need the most is a sense that there is an answer to the question: What are you doing now?"

Does Clark want to be a scout or coach some time in the future? He candidly admits he's not sure what he wants to do.

■ **CONT'D: Please see Clark/A2**

Fans jammed SaskPlace on Friday to join the Blades in saluting Wendel Clark

Wendel has thousands of new pen pals

By Doug McConachie
SP Sports Editor

There wasn't enough of Wendel Clark to go around. For the first time in recent memory, as many as 1,000 people stood outside SaskPlace waiting for the doors to open for a hockey game, waiting to join an autograph line that stretched five and six wide halfway around the concourse level of the 11,000-seat building, waiting to honour a player some describe as the best Saskatoon Blade ever.

They came with sticks and jerseys — not surprisingly, mostly Maple Leaf jerseys; Clark spent almost 13 seasons in Toronto. Others had hats and pictures and T-shirts, hoping for a signature from a favourite son who cut his junior hockey teeth in a Blades uniform from 1983 to 1985, then went on to the NHL for 15 years.

It was a night to honour a player who will always be a Saskatonian, city councillor and former Blades player Don Atchison said to the cheers of about 7,000. "You are the one who made hockey great."

No player, and there have been more than 1,000 WHLers who have gone on to be drafted by NHL teams, has shown more intensity and determination night in and night out, WHL commissioner Ron Robison observed.

No player showed greater "dignity, class . . . and a great deal of humility and dodged determindness," Blades president Jack Brodsky said as the team raised his No. 22 jersey to the rafters; the first time any Blade uniform has been retired.

Reanne Berry, 5, wasn't afraid to ask Wendel for his autograph, despite the fact she was wearing an Oilers sweater. Berry was accompanied by her parents, Greg and Gloria, and her 11-year-old brother Jayson.

They drove in from Young, almost an hour away, and made sure they were going to get Clark's autograph by arriving very early.

By 6:05 p.m. they and hundreds of others had surged through the doors.

There wasn't enough time for everyone to get his autograph, even though Clark was wristing them faster than any of the 330 regular-season goals he scored in the big league.

Sharol Fontana of Saskatoon had her two sons in tow and a brand new hockey stick with Wendel's name stamped on it, but that wasn't good enough.

"I want the real thing," she laughed.

Grey-haired Flo Petryshyn, with a small Leaf tattoo on her left cheek, confessed she was a Detroit Red Wings fan first, but Clark ranked right up there. She had his 2000 Red Wing hockey card for autographing.

Then for 30 minutes the crowd roared its approval and stood to honour Clark, a 35-year-old native of Kelvington who confessed to wishing he was playing instead of having to stand at centre ice during tributes from former players, coaches and broadcasters.

"I'm truly honoured," he told the fans. "It can't get any better than this."

Clark: Work ethic bred on farm

■ **Continued from A1**

He candidly admits he's not sure what he wants to do in the future. "Maybe some day I may say I really miss playing and the closest thing to playing is coaching. Maybe I'll stay in the office end of the team and do more marketing and PR. I'll wait and see what plays out."

Clark, who was traded to Quebec, the New York Islanders, Tampa Bay, Detroit and Chicago before finally being shipped back to Toronto, says he's especially pleased he ended his career with the same team he started with after being drafted first overall in 1985.

"I am pretty satisfied with my career. You always want to win a Stanley Cup, but I don't think I'd change anything else."

When he did retire, he ranked 17th in games played, seventh in goals, and 15th in points among all the players who ever wore the blue and white Maple Leaf. Each of these marks was second among Toronto left wingers to Hall of Famer Frank Mahovlich. He also ranked second among all Leafs in penalty minutes to Tiger Williams.

Throughout his Toronto career, Clark was arguably the favourite player among fans. But he never took it for granted.

"It's a relationship that the fans and I have had since I started here," he says. "At the end of the day, win or lose, what the fans like is players who show effort. They like to see effort."

Effort is something he has shown continually. Born in Kelvington in 1966, Clark's work ethic can be traced to his farming background and, in particular, to his parents Les and Alma Clark. The former Leaf captain is quick to assert that he "grew up playing one way and that's the way I played in minor hockey, in Saskatoon, and then here.

"When I first got to Saskatoon (in 1983) I had no idea that I would be drafted by the NHL in my second year. My biggest goal was to try to make the next best level, and it ended up being the NHL."

In those two years as a Blade, he scored 55 goals, added 100 assists and in his final junior year played on the gold-medal winning Canadian national team at the world junior championships.

A Career to Remember

On November 22, 2008, Wendel's banner was raised to the rafters of the Air Canada Centre.

I was really fortunate to have had so many amazing moments in my career. The ones which were most memorable, and the most meaningful, were with the Toronto Maple Leafs.

It began that very first day in June 1985, when the Leafs made me the No. 1 pick in the NHL Entry Draft. Then, of course, being named captain in 1991 was a big, big honour.

But, for me, the greatest honour of all was when they raised my banner at the Air Canada Centre. Just to be part of a group that included Johnny Bower, George Armstrong, Tim Horton, Darryl Sittler and the others was tremendous and truly humbling.

When Cliff Fletcher called that summer of 2008 and told me that "they were going to hang me from the rafters," I jokingly asked if there was a rope involved. I just couldn't believe it.

When you're going to be honoured like that, you suddenly spend a lot of time thinking back and remembering the good times and the bad times, the highs and lows of your career.

The day it was going to take place, I was kinda worried about what I was going to say and how I was going to say it. Because of all the emotions, the first thing I wanted to do was simply get through it without falling apart, to thank my wife, Denise, and the kids – Kylie, Kassie and Kody – who were down on the ice with me, and my Mom and Dad and my two brothers, who were watching from a private box upstairs. Somehow I managed. But it wasn't easy. So many times I came close to cracking.

The night was November 22, 2008, and it was more than just memorable. It was completely overwhelming for me and my family in every possible way. It's funny,

Wendel Clark NIGHT
Wendel Clark NIGHT
BMO Official bank of BE PROUD – GET LOUD! BMO
SMIRNOFF
ICE BOX
CLARK 17

when you're down there on the ice you hear the crowd much differently than when you're in a box or sitting in the seats. Standing there, the energy and the atmosphere of the crowd going nuts reminded me of how it felt and how it sounded during a game when I played.

During the ceremony, I couldn't stop from taking long, slow looks around the Air Canada Centre, just trying to soak up everything that I possibly could. All the emotions, so many powerful memories. This was my last hurrah and I wanted to savor that feeling one last time. It was so special.

In my speech, I deliberately avoided naming names. I knew if I did, emotionally it would be all over for me because I would have started thinking about each person and what they meant to me or had done for me, and I would have totally lost it and been unable to finish. I was fighting back the tears as it was.

In addition to being the greatest honour of my life, that evening also marked the closure of my NHL career.

It was also special for another reason. It was also the last thing my Dad ever saw involving me and the Maple Leafs. Two months later, in January, he passed away.

I don't know anybody who loved the game more than my Dad. I also didn't know that he had been a huge Maple Leafs fan long before they drafted me. In fact, the Leafs had always been his favourite team. But he never told me this until after I retired in 2000. That was my Dad. And that is when I realized how special it must have been for him to see me play at the Gardens, or sitting there watching a game from the "bunker" with Harold Ballard. That makes it even more special for me.

Speaking of Harold Ballard, he'd certainly have been high on that list of important people in my career whose names I didn't mention during my banner-raising ceremony at the ACC.

He was the one who pretty much demanded that the Leafs take me with the first pick in the 1985 draft.

Harold was the kind of guy who loved you one day and not so much the next. Although sometimes things seemed strained between us, in his final years we had a pretty good relationship.

Some of my best times involved several guys who were like brothers. In the 1980's it was guys like Todd Gill, Russ Courtnall and Gary Leeman (both Notre Dame Hounds alumni) and then later, in the 1990's, it would be Dave Ellett and Dougie Gilmour. We had so

CLARK
17
C
TORONTO MAPLE LEAFS
Wendel Clark NIGHT
THE KEG
STEAKHOUSE & BAR
PokerStars
BMO

much fun and they will be friends forever.

As for Cliff Fletcher, he was quite simply the most honourable man I ever met in hockey. There is nobody I admire or respect more in the game.

A guy you maybe never heard of, unless you were a diehard Leafs fan, is Chris Broadhurst. He was our athletic therapist and over the years I probably saw him more often than his wife. For a period of about six years, between 1988 and until I was traded in 1994, I literally spent four hours a day with him trying to deal with all of my injuries. And it was almost the same schedule in the summer. Chris' hard work kept me on the ice. Without him I would never have been able to play nearly as long as I did.

Last, but certainly not least, is Donnie Meehan. Not only do I think he's the best agent in the business, he's also been one of my best friends. We've been together since just before I was drafted. Whenever I needed some wise, sound and straight-shooting advice, he's the first guy I would go to. Always has been.

My greatest day in my career was getting drafted, because that started everything. My greatest year was 1985. It started with winning the gold medal at the World Junior Championship, finishing the season with the Saskatoon Blades, then the NHL draft in June, which changed my life forever.

Wendel was the 14th Leaf to be honoured with a banner hanging atop the ice of the Air Canada Centre. Dougie Gilmour's banner would be added three months later. The sweater numbers of two other Leaf players - Ace Bailey and Bill Barilko - have also been retired.

The high point came in October 1985 when I stepped on the ice at Maple Leaf Gardens and played my first game in the NHL as a Toronto Maple Leaf. Everything had led up to this point.

Some people have asked me about my greatest game in the NHL. When that topic comes up, some of them even mention that Game 6 in the playoffs against Los Angeles (in 1993). Honestly, it wasn't that big a deal for me, personally, because we lost to LA in overtime, 5-4. For me, winning was always what it was all about.

Not winning the Stanley Cup is by far the biggest disappointment of my career. It's what every NHL player dreams of doing. When you come as close to getting a shot at it as we did when the Leafs got to the semi-finals in 1993 and '94, well, it makes it harder.

I always wish I wasn't injured so often. But I guess that's the price you pay, when you're my size and play the

PokerStars
SPORTCHECK
IBM
CLARK
17
C
Ford
TORONTO MAPLE LEAFS

The Clark family was wowed by this memorable sight. His speech that night was brief and emotional.

on-the-edge style like I did. But that's the way I had to play. That's who I am.

But of all the questions I get and of all the conversations I have, probably 90 percent of them are about fights and fighting.

The first two NHL fights I ever had were on the second day of my first training camp with the Leafs – and they were with the same guy, Bob McGill. Funny, I remember getting a call from Donnie Meehan giving me a heads-up about McGill. Sure enough, Big Daddy and I go at it, not once, but twice, and on the same shift during an intra-squad game. Seems he was more interested in my penalty minutes with Saskatoon than he was with the fact that I'd been drafted No. 1. So he wanted to formally welcome me to the Leafs. As I would find out later when the season started, it was nice having Big Daddy on your side.

Once we left training camp, my first two fights in a game were with Marty McSorley. The first was in an exhibition game in Edmonton. I was right beside the Oilers bench, when the door swung open and I kind of fell on top of him. I can't remember the second time we fought, but it doesn't matter, because Marty and I used to drop the gloves in just about every third game we played against each other.

Everybody asks who the toughest player was I ever fought. And the answer's easy. There was no one toughest. When you're a middleweight like I was, and you're in a world of heavyweights like Marty McSorley or Bob Probert, or Behn Wilson, who was definitely the meanest, trust me, they are all very, very tough. Being the team "policeman" is a really hard job that only a few players can do and even fewer want to do it. (I didn't mention my cousin, Joey Kocur, because the question was who was the toughest I "ever fought," and Joey and I never did fight.)

As I've already mentioned, I started fighting in Junior at Saskatoon. I remember one game, we were down to three defencemen and the coach had told me not to fight. One guy on the other team was really coming after me all night and I couldn't do anything about it. But Joey Kocur could and he destroyed the poor guy. That was the only time I was ever going to let someone else fight my battles for me. Since then, nobody ever did. When I was named top defenceman in the West, I had 253 minutes in penalties.

Like I said earlier, playing on the edge was the only

way I knew. Nobody ever forced me to play that way. It's how I wanted to play and how I enjoyed playing – and it came natural.

It also creates space for you, which a power forward like me had to do. By doing a little something crazy, it can create space, and you put fear into an opposing player at the same time. Guys like Alex Ovechkin, Sidney Crosby and Evgeni Malkin create the same fear, but they do it with pure talent. I obviously wasn't as skilled as guys like them, so I had to do it my way, by being in your face and never backing down.

When you play that style, you're going to catch guys the wrong way sometimes. I'm talking about guys who aren't known for their aggressiveness and toughness. When that happens, you can expect a little payback. For example, if I hit Marty Howe, somebody who's not a fighter but one of the team's best players, you just knew their tough guy would be coming after me.

So I knew I would be dealing with a lot of those guys if I continued to play physical. Prior to the instigator penalty in 1992, if I wanted to run around and play physical but didn't want to fight, an opposing player could still grab me and beat on me and only get a couple of minutes in penalties.

The referee would say, "You're an idiot and you stirred the pot, so you'd better stand up for what you did."

It's not that way today. Back then, I either had to stop running around or answer for it.

The way the game's played now, I could run around all night and nobody would stop me. I wouldn't have to answer the bell to anybody. The hitting is now more dangerous than ever. The game no longer polices itself, which is why I think the game was much safer when I played than it is today.

I remember back early in my career, we had a line brawl with Edmonton. Glen Sather got mad at me because I grabbed Craig MacTavish, who wasn't a fighter. What Sather didn't know was that when it started I had told Craig, "If you don't swing, there won't be a fight. So don't take a swing." And what does MacTavish do? Well, he throws a punch. And I started giving it back to him until the linesmen jumped in. Now, if I'd been a 29-year old veteran, all I would have probably done was take Craig to the ice and keep him there until all the crazy stuff was over. But at age 19, I just flipped the switch.

One thing I've never been able to understand is why teams keep around old tough guys. They only fight when they have to fight. And the older you get, as a hockey player, the less you want to do it and the harder it is to flip the switch. It's even harder when nobody did anything to you. When you're 30 or 31, have a wife and family at home, you're mind-set is much different than it is for some 21-year-old enforcer. When you are 21, you can be mad for no reason at all.

I always got as much of a high out of a good hit as a good punch. And I've had a few big hits during my career, but I guess, the biggest took place one night in St. Louis. I really leveled Bruce Bell behind the net and knocked him out cold. I caught him not looking and with his head down. Sure, it was a hard hit, but it was also a clean hit, where my shoulder made contact with his head. I was never a headhunter. But if it had happened today, I'd be suspended. They don't allow a check like that anymore.

I've also been involved with my share of bench-clearing brawls over the years. But I guess the craziest was against the Detroit Red Wings. In that game I ran right over Barry Melrose behind the net and we both got penalties. As we headed for the penalty box, Joey Kocur jumped over the boards, which meant everybody else on both teams also came over the boards. So here we were: three cousins from Kelvington, starting one of the last bench-clearing, free-for-alls in the NHL.

And maybe the funniest story where fighting was concerned happened in the 1994 playoffs and involved the San Jose Sharks' Jamie Baker. Jamie was a big-time yapper and an agitator, whose job was to stir things up.

Early in the series he finally got me so mad that I wanted to tear his head off. He just kept going at me, until I was ready to snap and let him have it. Then I realized he was playing me perfectly, trying to get me to do something stupid.

Before a faceoff, I skated over to him and said, "I'm not going to talk to you or look at you the rest of this series. I don't want to even know who you are. But there's something you should know. Whenever we play the Sharks next season, I am either going to spear you or one-punch you every single shift of every single game. I will take a stupid penalty in the regular season, but I'm not taking one in the playoffs. So have your fun now because you're not going to have any when I get a hold of you next season."

I never heard so much as peep from him again in the series.

After the banner-raising ceremony, Wendel drops the puck in an honourary faceoff with Chicago's Jonathan Toews and Toronto's Tomas Kaberle.

Every player remembers his first game in the NHL. In mine, I was on a line with Rick Vaive and Bill Derlago playing against the Boston Bruins. During the game, Billy set me up so often I should have had three goals. Instead I didn't get any. So what happens right after the game, Billy is traded to the Bruins for Tom Fergus. Since then, I've always kidded Billy D that if I'd scored on one of his passes, maybe he wouldn't have been traded.

My first NHL goal finally came in my third NHL game. It was against Chicago. The Blackhawks' goalie was Murray Bannerman and I actually scored twice that night. Both of them were on goal-mouth scrambles around the Chicago net. They were garbage goals – but these count just as much as the ones that make TV sports highlight reels.

There is no place in the NHL like Toronto. During my 15 years of playing pro hockey, I played for six different teams and in every rink in the NHL. Toronto really is the centre of the hockey universe.

They call Detroit "Hockeytown," but if you're a player, Toronto really is the place to be. Having played for both the Leafs and the Red Wings I can say this.

For example, Stevie Yzerman is a legend in the Motor City. But as popular as he is, he can still go out at night for dinner or a movie or even go shopping at the malls and not be bothered by anyone.

However, if Stevie ever had the same kind of career in Toronto, he would have needed a 12-foot fence around his home for privacy and be surrounded by a group of bodyguards when he went out in public. Of course, I'm exaggerating a bit, but just to show the difference between a player in Detroit and being one in Toronto. In my opinion, hockey in Toronto is a much bigger part of everyday life than it is in Detroit.

When I arrived in Toronto for my rookie season in 1985, it had a small town feeling to it. I lived downtown, not far from the Gardens, and everything revolved around that hub area. Cheap cab fares got you pretty much everywhere and that made the city seem not so big.

Just like in Kelvington or any small town, everybody knew who you were and waved or asked how things were going. But also like in Kelvington, if you messed up, they knew that, too. Toronto's still like that today. When you're a Maple Leaf, you can go absolutely anywhere, a restaurant or store or a party, and not only feel welcome, but in most cases, they make you feel like a king.

My life after hockey has been great. Darryl Sittler and I are team ambassadors for the Leafs. We do a lot of public relations work; meet fans and corporate sponsors, make charity appearances on behalf of the Leafs. It keeps us connected to the game, but not on a day-to-day basis, so we can do other things business-wise and spend more time with the family.

I once thought about coaching or working in the hockey department. But in today's game, that means you're going to be involved in what you're doing 24/7. And after spending 15 years like that, Denise and the kids deserve to have me around for them.

My schedule lets me do a lot more family functions, which I enjoy, but missed a lot of them in the past. I'm also very involved with our restaurants and promotional work for companies like ClubLink, National Sports, Oakville Chevrolet and Naka. Plus, as I mentioned I am involved with several charities. So my life stays pretty busy, which is the way I like it.

You know, on that November evening back in 2008, when they raised my banner at the ACC, well, later, after the excitement had died down and everything was over, I took the time to really look back at my hockey career. I tried to step back and really think about what I had done and how I had done it. You know, I felt pretty good about it. I felt good that I had left it all on the line. I felt good that I had given everything my body would let me give. I felt good that I had done it from the first time I laced up the skates to the last.

When your NHL career is finally over, you just hope you played the game and conducted yourself in a way that was respected and trusted by the guys you played with, and against. For me it was always what the players thought that mattered most because they're the ones who really know you best, and what you're really all about.

So, if they looked at you and saw a good, honest teammate, then you've had a pretty good career. For a farm boy from Kelvington, that was the ultimate honor.

ABOVE: Wendel poses in an ad with Oakville Chevrolet's Hass Hijazi (left) and Craig Taylor (right), the dealership's sales manager. BELOW: Wendel also serves as a pitchman for Naka Nutritional Products and other companies.

LEFT: Wendel and Rob Cheevers, ClubLink's Manager of Special Events and Business Development.
RIGHT: Tim Green, ClubLink's Executive Director of Sales and Marketing, and Wendel.

WENDEL CLARK CAREER STATS

			REGULAR SEASON					PLAYOFFS				
Season	**Team**	**LGE**	**GP**	**G**	**A**	**Pts.**	**PIM**	**GP**	**G**	**A**	**Pts.**	**PIM**
1983-84	Saskatoon Blades	WHL	72	23	45	68	225	-	-	-	-	-
1984-85	Saskatoon Blades	WHL	64	32	55	87	253	3	3	3	6	7
1985-86	Toronto Maple Leafs	NHL	66	34	11	45	227	10	5	1	6	47
1986-87	Toronto Maple Leafs	NHL	80	37	23	60	271	13	6	5	11	38
1987-88	Toronto Maple Leafs	NHL	28	12	11	23	80	-	-	-	-	-
1988-89	Toronto Maple Leafs	NHL	15	7	4	11	66	-	-	-	-	-
1989-90	Toronto Maple Leafs	NHL	38	18	8	26	116	5	1	1	2	19
1990-91	Toronto Maple Leafs	NHL	63	18	16	34	152	-	-	-	-	-
1991-92	Toronto Maple Leafs	NHL	43	19	21	40	123	-	-	-	-	-
1992-93	Toronto Maple Leafs	NHL	66	17	22	39	193	21	10	10	20	51
1993-94	Toronto Maple Leafs	NHL	64	46	30	76	115	18	9	7	16	24
1994-95	Quebec Nordiques	NHL	37	12	18	30	45	6	1	2	3	6
1995-96	New York Islanders	NHL	58	24	19	43	60	-	-	-	-	-
1995-96	Toronto Maple Leafs	NHL	13	8	7	15	16	6	2	2	4	2
1996-97	Toronto Maple Leafs	NHL	65	30	19	49	75	-	-	-	-	-
1997-98	Toronto Maple Leafs	NHL	47	12	7	19	80	-	-	-	-	-
1998-99	Tampa Bay Lightning	NHL	65	28	14	42	35	-	-	-	-	-
1998-99	Detroit Red Wings	NHL	12	4	2	6	2	10	2	3	5	10
1999-00	Chicago Blackhawks	NHL	13	2	0	2	13	-	-	-	-	-
1999-00	Toronto Maple Leafs	NHL	20	2	2	4	21	6	1	1	2	4
	NHL Totals	NHL	793	330	234	564	1690	95	37	32	69	201

Wendel Clark Muscles Into GTA Bar Biz Scene

By Kim Honey
The Toronto Star
Jan. 23, 2008

Wendel Clark is in affable mode, chatting up people at the new restaurant that bears his name at the AMC Plaza in Vaughan.

A hint of the old scrapper flashes across his face when the former Maple Leafs captain is asked to pose with yet another Wendel Burger. A grimace, and then it's gone.

The problem is the burger is made from half a pound of beef and stretches about four inches high thanks to some very thick onion rings piled on top of the double smoked bacon and three kinds of cheddar. And he already had one for lunch.

Clark manhandles the 'burg, mashing it down to a manageable size and putting the heart clogger to his mouth.

"It's only got three calories," he jokes.

Downtown Toronto has its Wayne Gretzky's, and the burbs have their Don Cherry's. But the owners of the new Wendel Clark's Classic Grill and Sports Lounge are banking on the retired hockey star's mass appeal to attract a crowd in Vaughan.

The contract with Dynamic Hospitality and Entertainment Group, which owns and operates the Atlantis Pavilion at Ontario Place, Yuk Yuk's and the Eglinton Grand, calls for visits a few times a year. But since Clark gets a cut of the revenue, "the better the place does, the better he does," says Sam D'Uva, the company's managing director.

And Clark, who lives 10 minutes away in King City, says he plans to stop by every week or two. "More than Wayne (drops in at Gretzky's)," he points out. "I've got a closer commute."

At home, Clark enjoys his wife's cooking, and the family favourite is shepherd's pie. He loves to grill meat on his Weber barbecue and he'll be shopping for a new one soon, once he finishes the new cottage he's building in Muskoka.

"We do a lot of steak, a lot of filet mignon, tenderloin rolls." To his chagrin, one of his daughters doesn't like meat. But there are no special concessions.

"They eat what everybody's eating or they go hungry." Um, okay, Dad. You don't argue with a man who amassed a total of 1,690 penalty minutes during his NHL career. That was over 793 regular season games, mind you.

His favourite restaurant back then was Gibson's Steakhouse in Chicago, where he would always order the same thing: the 16- or 18-ounce New York striploin.

"I was younger then. I could eat a lot," says the 41-year-old. "I wouldn't even try that now. We have a nice (steak) at the restaurant that's 14 ounces."

At his new restaurant in Vaughan, Ont., Wendel samples the famous half-pound hamburger.

When he is reminded a typical portion of protein is no more than 3 ounces in weight, he laughs. "That's why I eat it standing up."

The restaurant is designed to be "a step above the usual sports bar," with food comparable to the higher-end chains such as The Keg and Canyon Creek.

Executive chef David Copperthwaite may have all the old sports bar standbys on the menu – chicken wings, nachos and caesar salad – but everything has a twist. Poutine is served with goat's cheese and peppercorn gravy, the nachos have ground bison on top (a nod to Clark's Saskatchewan roots), and the deconstructed caesar salad features a thin slice of baguette fit into a muffin tin and toasted. The bread cylinder is stuffed with hearts of romaine, scattered with bacon and adorned with slivers of asiago cheese. Anchovies come on the side.

Instead of salmon, the old standby, he buys blue marlin from Costa Rica.

One of the toughest things to torque is the good old french fry, and Copperthwaite cuts his into matchsticks, fries them till they're crisp, then tosses them with a mixture of chili, roasted garlic and a little sugar.

"They're addictive," he says. "It's the key. If you're going to make a burger, make good fries."

OUR FIRST COLLEGE FOOTBALL PREVIEW ISSUE

MVP
CANADA'S SPORTS MAGAZINE
SEPTEMBER/OCTOBER, 1986 $2.50

IS MATT DUNIGAN A BETTER QB THAN ROY DEWALT? NOPE!

TERRY PUHL: MAJOR LEAGUE BASEBALL'S LONE STAR CANADIAN

ANICK GRAVELINE: STRIVING TO BE WORLD'S BEST SAILBOARD RACER

THE KING AND THE KID

"Wendel Clark? He plays just like Charlie Conacher"

09
0 55113 70150

The King & the Kid

By Gare Joyce
MVP Magazine, April 1986

It's 10:30, well before the lunch rush at the Hot Stove Club. Tucked away on the Church Street side of Maple Leaf Gardens, the bistro acts as the exclusive refuge for the brass and troops enlisted with the blue and white. It is a place for a hockey Legion, for servicemen and vets to grab a bite and swap war stories. The patrons opt for the Hot Stove because their celebrity obstructs dining at Winston's, Fenton's or other classy mess halls. Joe Fan will be turned away politely should he walk in from Church Street.

Those who enjoy Hot Stove privileges rarely enter from the street. They come from a labyrinth of concealed hallways, hidden stairways and sidedoors.

Francis Michael (King) Clancy, decked out in a gray flannel suit and a blue tie flecked with maple leafs, negotiates a set of stairs closeted at the back door of the Hot Stove kitchen.

"Hiya boys," Clancy says to two cooks.

"Hyello Meester Clancy," one says. "Joo' like toast today?"

"Toast sounds great," says Clancy, the vice president of MLG Inc.

"Joo' going to the track later Meester Clancy?"

"Jee-sus I gotta. The other day I wanted to put a bet down out at Woodbine. I liked this horse a lot. But I get talking to some guy, I dunno who. At the track these guys think I know them. Anyway, I talk to this sonvobitch so long that I don't have time to get a bet down. I would have won two grand. So I gotta go back there."

Though hardly balletic, Clancy walks with a jauntier step than most octogenarian gents. He shuffles into the dining room. He'd be tap-dancing if that clown hadn't stalled him on his way to the ticket window.

"Hiya doing' boys," Clancy says to the floor general and his squad of waiters,

"Good, how are you?" the manager replies in kind, knowing that Clancy never stops at "Good."

"Jee-sus I's stiff. Hadda drive out to Kingston yesterday. Ballard's not here so I guess that leaves me in charge."

"King, there's a writer here to see you."

"Aaa-aww, okay. Where is he?" A Jee-sus dread crosses Clancy's face. "How are ya? Lissen, ask me about stuff that happened 60 years ago. I can't remember what happened last week. What d'ya have in mind, son?"

Here stands history, King Clancy. In the 1920's he made headlines when NHL wars were waged on outdoor rinks and natural ice. As a rookie with the Ottawa Senators he roomed with Frank Nighbor, the man who invented the poke check. Clancy was already a veteran when the Gardens, this very building, opened shop in 1931. When his playing days ended he refereed and coached. Here sits a man whose popularity and gift of gab haven't eroded through 83 full and antic years, a man who signed a 10-year contract at age 80 if only to keep his lifetime options open.

"Well, sir, Wendel Clark is coming by," the writer says, extending a hand. "I thought the three of us would sit down, have lunch and talk about hockey."

"Wendel is a good kid," Clancy says, as he pulls up a chair.

"How are you today?" the writer asks as Clancy slowly folds himself into his seat.

"Stiff as hell. I hadda drive out to Kingston yesterday. Bill Cook died. You didn't know Bill Cook did ya?"

"Bill and Bun Cook, the Rangers," the writer says, exhausting his working knowledge on the subject.

"Yeah. Bill Cook was even older than me – 90. The toughest right winger I played against. Jee-sus ya didn't wanna mess with him. In Madison Square Garden they had chicken wire instead of glass behind the goals. One game I hit Bunnie Cook so hard behind the net that I knocked him upside down. He was hanging upside down, skates caught in the chicken wire! I was standing back, admiring my work, when all of a sudden it feels like a beam came down on my head. Next thing, the ref is askin' me how many fingers he's holding up and Bill Cook's standing over me, smiling."

Storyteller *sui generis*. He comes by his anecdotal

prowess honestly – his father was born in County Cork, as Irish as Paddy's pig. One might consider Clancy's style elliptical. Nothing could be further from the truth. When he seems to drift off topic, without warning, he returns with a concise denouement, the moral of the story emphatic in its bluntness. And though Clancy was an all-star defenceman, a prodigious scorer for a blueliner, he inevitably casts himself in these stories as a klutz and, at best, an average guy along for the ride."You know I never could fight worth a damn. Had hundreds of fights, never won one of them. Okay I might get a punch in if a guy was already down. I'd give them a lick like that. But I was a small guy, 150 pounds. I gave the tough guys as much of a fight as a punching bag."

The likelihood is that Clancy won a few fights but loveable losers always win audiences. King is asked if he ever suffered injuries.

"I never thought I could get hurt. I was knocked out a bunch of times but that doesn't hurt. I lost a bunch of my teeth, had my nose broke, cuts, broke my hands, fingers; but no, it never entered my mind that I could get hurt. I was on the ice the night in Boston when Eddie Shore cracked Ace Bailey's skull and ended Ace's career. But it didn't bother or scare me. I felt sorry for Bailey because he was a game player, but I thought it could never happen to me."

Clancy says he respected Bailey but he leaves the impression that he was closer to other players on the Leaf team.

"When Mr. Smythe bought me from the Ottawas, Toronto had a great bunch of young guys, just like this team today. I had two great friends, Hap Day and Charlie Conacher.

"Hap Day was a great defenceman and a college man. He didn't talk a lot but everything made sense. You could tell that he would be a great coach and he was. He understood the game and he'd communicate it.

"Charlie was my best friend. A great right winger and scorer. Tough as hell. He was a young lion, a battler. If you got in a squabble he'd be the first one there. He was a great athlete, could've played in the CFL if he wanted. He was probably a better footballer than his brother, Lionel. Charlie and I would always go out. He was the type of guy everybody could take to. He was different than me. I've never had a drink in my life – that's why I'm still moping around here. I would go out and drink ginger out and Charlie would have a few drinks, getting into all kinds of jackpots. He enjoyed living a little faster than me, but I enjoyed watching him in action – on and off the ice."

Clancy's voice fades to a whisper, a faint echo of a band interrupted by Charlie's death almost 19 years ago. "He was a great, great friend.

"How you doin' son?" Clancy asks a blue-jeaned 19-year-old Clark.

The most exciting rookie in Toronto since Teeder Kennedy in the 1940's, the object of the most fanatical hockey idolatry in this city since the coming of Francis Michael Clancy himself, Wendel Clark, as wide set and solid as a combine harvester, shakes King's hand and pulls up a seat at the table.

As Clark sits, one appreciates the breadth of time here spanned. Clancy could be Clark's great-grandfather. Four generations of Leafs.

"I had to drive out to Kingston yesterday for Bill Cook's funeral," King says to Wendel. "You wouldn't know Bill Cook. But Kingston's a long enough drive for me anyway."

"I'm going to take three days driving out to Kelvington."

"Three days to Saskatchewan?"

"Yeah, I'll visit friends on the way," the laconic Clark says.

"It's too bad you kids didn't get by St. Louis, 'cause I thought you'd win the Cup if you beat the Blues. I really did. You boys were generally coming on at the finish."

To Clark this bares a wound that's barely had time to heal. In the fifth game of the division final he rattled a shot off the post. Had that shot gone in, it's likely the Leafs would have advanced by the Blues to the conference final against Calgary. "Well, next year," he offers.

"I'll have some soup. Wendel, you should have something," Clancy suggests.

"I'll have a steak sandwich," the young Leaf phenom states.

"This young man is really going to be something," Clancy begins with theatrical flourish. "I just hope you have a long sojourn 'cause in one season you've made a name for yourself in this town."

Clancy offers up platitudes and kudos for Clark, but one can sense that these men embody different times, different attitudes and temperaments.

During his 13-year tenure in Toronto, Wendel scored a total of 205 goals and had 1,062 penalty minutes. King Clancy (right) would score 52 of his 137 NHL goals while playing for the Leafs.

The sandwich and soup soon arrive and the talk turns to turning pro and their first games.

"My first game ..." Clark begins, recalling that time oh-so many weeks ago. "I first thought about playing in the NHL when I was in junior in Saskatoon. Playing in the NHL became my goal as soon as I thought it might happen. I didn't think about the first game much when I stepped on the ice. I'm not sure who we played. In the warm-up I thought about how I used to watch the NHL and now I was in it. But as soon as the puck was dropped I just stopped thinking about it. Some guys try to adjust to the NHL and they get away from the things they've done all of their lives. I went out and played the game just like I did in junior or midget. When my career's over I'll think about it more."

"The kids are too caught up to realize what's going on around them," Clancy breaks in. He has had 65 years to ruminate over and crystallize the memory of his maiden outing. "My first pro game was Frank Boucher's first as well. Ottawa vs. Hamilton, in Hamilton. Frank and I didn't play until the game went into overtime. Mr. Green, the coach, put Frank and I on in the overtime and I scored a goal. To this day it didn't go in. It went through the side of the net, but the referee didn't catch it – and we won."

"Funny how I signed," Clancy continues, his tomato soup half-eaten and cooling. "I was playing for St. Brigid's School in Ottawa. No scouts, no drafts, no lawyers back then. Only four teams in the NHL. I had no idea anybody had watched me play. I went to Mr. Gorman, the owner of the Senators, and he had a stack of 100 one-dollar bills on his desk. He said, 'Sign with the Senators and I'll give you this money.' I'd never given pro hockey a thought of it until he offered the contract. The stack looked like an awful lot considering I had 15 cents in my pocket. I went home and asked what to do. He wasn't sure I could play. My friends convinced me I should try. I got a salary of $800 a year and the $100 bonus, which I gave to my mum."

Clark prefers not to vouchsafe the precise dollar value

THE KING AND THE KID

shifting his silverware. "When I played with Ottawa, I lived with my folks and worked as a customs officer. But when I got to Toronto I stayed at the best hotel in North America. It cost me $1.33 a day, 33 bucks a month. A bunch of us stayed there. We thought we'd gone to heaven. Back then I was making $8,500 a year, plus a bonus of $1,500 – the league was bigger and so was the money.

Back in my day there were great players y'know. Newsy LaLonde, Sprague Cleghorn and Joe Malone – he scored 44 goals in 20 games. These guys were tough as hell. They'd leather you, no matter who you were. Who impresses you, Wendel?"

Clark hesitates. He lays down his sandwich. "Bernie Federko is a great player," he says. "Five or six guys in Edmonton have great skill. But you can't be 'impressed.' If you are just looking, you stop playing. You'll get beat if you're impressed. I go out and say 'I dare you to beat me. You'll get beat if you're impressed. I go out and say, 'I dare you to beat me. You'll have to go through me to score.' You have to put yourself on their level. If they have more skill, then you just have to work harder."

of his contract nor its incentive clauses. "I did not have much to do with the negotiations for my contract," he explained. "I play hockey and my agent, Don Meehan, looks after the business end. He set me up living in Toronto living with the folks of Peter Zezel (of the Philadelphia Flyers). That made life easy. It's good to have a family at the rink and when you leave the rink. It's tough enough to start in the NHL as well as look for an apartment. You can't play your best living in a hotel."

"In my first year in Toronto I stayed at the Royal York Hotel," says Clancy, his soup now finished, nervously

"Sounds a lot like Charlie Conacher," Clancy enthuses. "That's why I like Wendel. He's got the same attitude as Charlie. Plays like him. The Hound Line and the Kid Line are a lot alike. And he's good people. A tough guy, but a good, fun-loving kid off the ice."

Clark's not uncomfortable with the comparison. Like Bill Cook, Charlie Conacher wasn't one of Clark's boyhood favourites. Conacher played long before Clark stepped on the ice.

Less flattering comparisons have been made in the media. One Toronto writer compared young Clark to

Reggie Fleming. Like Fleming, Clark is short on the game's nuances but long on strength, rage and malevolence. Though Clark at 19 is several times the player Fleming ever was, the young man takes no offence at the slight. He doesn't precisely understand it. Even Reggie Fleming was before Clark's time.

"I'm used to dealing with the press," the youngster says. "In the west, junior hockey is on the front page of the sports section. In the east, the press doesn't bother with it that much. I don't let the press get under my skin at all.

"While I can give it 100 percent, I'll stay in the game. I don't think I'll ever go into coaching. But, at 19, you don't think about the end of your career." He speaks the last sentence as if dispassionately distanced, as if reflecting on another player's career.

Sixty-five years ago King Clancy was of a like mind. No idea of the events that would follow. No idea that he'd bury Bill Cook and many friends and family. No idea that he'd outlive his beloved, Rachel. No idea that he'd become the most enduring and lovable character in Canadian sports.

"Never in Gawd's world did I imagine I'd be in the game so long. It's been good to me. Toronto's been good to me. I quit playin' when it quit bein' fun. Nothing else – money, fame – nothing figured in it. Bein' 'round the Gardens is fun. The people here in the offices, in the Hot Stove, Mr. Ballard, the players, the coaches; they're so good to me. I'll quit being' 'round here if it isn't fun, but that'll never happen.

"It gets a little lonely sometimes, watching my friends passing on, but the Gardens and the kids like Wendel keep me young. Mr. Ballard and I are no spring chickens, but we have our laughs."

Clark smiles. Clancy isn't fiddling with his silverware anymore. His voice loudens as if to defend his involvement *simper fidelis* with the Leafs, but nothing here requires the sanction of the writer. The Gardens, that shrine for hockey, has become a hotbed of controversy for reporters, but not even the most cold-blooded of their numbers could rail against Francis Michael Clancy. He stands above their bleatings.

It seems the right point to grab the tab and get a photo of King and Wendel. They are led to the anteroom of the Lounge.

The studio lights burn. Clancy's incandescent smile compels the photographer to close the lens a stop. The man behind the camera says Clancy has a future as a male model. "You'll put Ron Duguay out of business."

"I couldn't stand the cut in pay," Clancy says, never missing a beat as the shots are banged off at machine-gun speed.

The vanity session lasts but 10 minutes. They head out to the hallway and the front door of the Gardens. Clancy walks by the gallery of Stanley Cup-winning Leafs teams. An identical picture of Clancy appears in the display of the 1963 and '64 teams.

"See that," he says. "Ageless."

A kindergarten class is taking a tour of the Gardens. Though they've never seen an NHL game, the children can sense with the intuitive intelligence of youth that these two men aren't mere passers-by.

"Who's that?" asks a tow-headed boy pointing at the more venerable gentleman.

"Children, this is King Clancy. Say hello," the teacher instructs.

"Hi kids! Howya doin'? Why don't I come out and visit ya?"

"Hi King. Hello King."

"Are you really a king? What are you king of?"

Wendel Clark looks on, amused but bushed by the trials of a long season and newfound celebrity. Clancy is child-eyed, smiling among the horde of youngsters. Clark, a three-day drive from home, a time zone away from his own childhood, stands off to one side, more distant.

"Who's that guy, King?"

"That's Wendel Clark, kids. He's a great hockey player for the Leafs."

Stiffly, a little formally, Clark waves.

"Hi kids," he says, fighting over the words like an actor struggling with a script.

"Clancy could stay with the kids all day. Maybe one of these five-year-olds will be wearing a Leaf uniform in 14 years?

At 12:15 it was time for Clancy and Clark to cut out. Clark will drive out to Kelvington and his parents' grain farm; Clancy out to Woodbine and a different set of four- and five-year-olds.

The young man and the old boy step out onto Carlton Street, marching into the Yonge Street horizon. Traffic stops. Horns blare.

The Nightmare Off the Ice

By Tom Jones
St. Petersburg Times, January 22, 1999

First and foremost, Tampa Bay Lightning All-Star Wendel Clark is a grateful father. Hockey was Wendel Clark's life until he realized life was more important than hockey.

His lesson came during the wee hours of Feb. 16, 1996. As he watched doctors frantically trying to save the life of his newborn daughter, his first child, Clark realized hockey wasn't everything he thought it was.

Even now, during Clark's comeback season in which he will represent the Lightning in Sunday's All-Star Game at the Ice Palace, Clark knows what matters. And it isn't hockey.

"I used to think I had been in some tough situations in hockey, big games, whatever," Clark said. "Looking back now, I know that when you really get down to it, it really doesn't matter as much as you thought it did.

"That night changed everything."

The pregnancy was normal. "I was as healthy as a horse," Denise Clark said.

No problems, no worries. Denise checked into a Long Island hospital, just down the road from where the Islanders, Clark's team, played. The baby was arriving three weeks early, but she had good size: 6 pounds, 5 ounces. The delivery was smooth.

Until the final two minutes. Denise was heavily medicated; she had no idea there were problems. Wendel, though, knew something had gone terribly wrong. "All of a sudden, they're calling for doctors, nurses, all kinds of people," Wendel said. "Basically, there's no other way to put it: She was born dead."

During the final stages of delivery, the baby began hemorrhaging from the brain. A sac, nearly as big as the head itself, began filling with blood.

Meantime, the umbilical cord started to wrap around the baby's throat. When doctors cut the cord, nearly all the baby's blood rushed into Denise's placenta.

For nearly five minutes, doctors could not find a pulse on the baby. Wendel put on his best face and assured Denise things were fine. But even in her hazy state, Denise sensed things were not fine. Doctors had no choice but to begin a transfusion using Denise's blood.

One problem: Denise's blood did not match the baby's.

"They didn't believe it would work," Denise said. "It was a total last resort. But it was either that or she was going to die. The head of the medical team made the decision. Really, there was no other choice. There was no time to do anything else."

The transfusion worked temporarily. The baby was revived, but she had to be moved immediately to a neonatal clinic in New York City. And less than 10 hours after delivering her baby, an exhausted Denise checked out of the Long Island hospital.

"I had to be with my daughter," she said.

The Clarks named the girl Kylie Lee. They had her christened.

For the next three days, Kylie clung to life. Several times doctors feared she was about to die, but each time she battled back. "I was a total basket case," Denise said. "Wendel, though, was a rock. He talked to the doctors. He understands all the medical stuff. He made all the decisions. I don't know how I could have done it without him. He got me through it."

Hardly anyone in hockey, including Wendel's coach and teammates, knew much about the Clarks' nightmare. Wendel said little, but when he did, it was very matter-of-fact: She may not make it. It's touch and go. We'll see.

He would show up for practice, for games, then head back to the city to be with Denise and Kylie.

The worst part, the Clarks said, was that they couldn't touch Kylie. They could only look at her through a pane of glass.

Kylie and Denise joined Wendel in Toronto after she was finally released from the New York hospital in 1996.

"She had this sac (from the hemorrhage) hanging from her head, so she had to be kept real still," Denise said. "It was so sad. She was so little. She was in so much pain. No one really could touch her."

"I think it was much harder on my wife than me," Wendel said. "You know how it is between mother and daughter. And for her not to be able to hold the baby was tough, real tough."

Kylie began rejecting her mother's blood. She turned severely jaundiced. More transfusions were done. Several times in the three days after the birth, doctors put the Clarks on alert: Kylie might not make it. "But she was such a little fighter," Denise said. "The doctors would say, 'Okay, if she doesn't start improving by, say, midnight, then we have to take action.' Then at 11 o'clock, she would make a turn for the better. That kept happening over and over."

Kylie kept fighting. A week went by. Then the Clarks were thrown another curve. Wendel was traded.

The good thing was that he was traded to Toronto. Clark knew Toronto well; he had played there for nine years before being traded to Quebec in 1994 and the Islanders a year later. And Toronto has an excellent reputation for children's hospitals. But Clark left Long Island without Denise and Kylie, who continued her fight for life.

The fight was successful. After 3½ weeks, Kylie had fully recovered and was released from the hospital. Mother finally held daughter. And the next day, the Clarks were reunited in Toronto.

Kylie is fine now. For the first year she had to be checked thoroughly every three months. Doctors couldn't be sure if she had sustained brain damage from the ordeal. But nearly three years later, she appears to be in normal health.

"She bounces off the walls, runs, plays, does all the things a 3-year-old does," Wendel said. "If you didn't know what happened, then you wouldn't know what happened."

Last year the Clarks had another daughter, Kassidy. She was delivered by Caesarean section – doctors wanted to do what they could to avoid the problems Kylie had because they still don't know what happened the night she was born.

Clark doesn't talk about the ordeal unless asked. He doesn't say much about anything unless asked. He's private but not rude. He's quiet but not boring. He's just a normal country boy from Kelvington, Saskatchewan (pop. 1,000). He doesn't have much to say about Kylie's medical problems because the way he sees it, everyone goes through tough family times. What makes hockey players so special?

But don't believe for a second the ordeal hasn't changed him. "You can't possibly be the same person after that," Clark said. "Let's just say it gets your priorities in order. Hockey is just hockey, it's not life and death."

Kylie taught her father that.

Special Memories of the Clark Family

Wendel and Denise Clark were married on June 29th, 1996 in Saskatoon, Sask. The band at their wedding reception included several close hockey friends such as Beeker and Dave Ellett.

ABOVE: During 13 seasons in Toronto, Wendel became a favourite with the local media. **RIGHT:** Dick Beddoes, a sportswriter for The Globe and Mail, poses for a photo with Wendel at Maple Leaf Gardens.

TOP: Alma Clark (left) and Rita Kocur (Joey Kocur's mom) enjoy a cup of coffee together and the opportunity to discuss their boys' hockey careers. **ABOVE:** Kelly Chase and Wendel. **LEFT:** The Leafs' dapper new star is spotted on a night out in chilly downtown Toronto.

ABOVE: Les and Alma Clark view an exhibit at the Hockey Hall of Fame which includes their son's 1985 World Junior Hockey Championship jersey. **LEFT:** The Clarks pose with the Stanley Cup during the trophy's visit to Saskatchewan.

Wendel and his two daughters, Kassie (left) and Kylie.

TOP: Kylie (left), Kody and Kassie in a fun family photo after Wendel returned to Toronto in 2000. **LEFT:** Kylie and Kassie (right) dressed in their Detroit Red Wings' sweaters, with their father's Number (71). **ABOVE:** Wendel with Kassie (right) and her friend, Kennedy Cullen, at a Tampa Bay Lightning Christmas party in 1998. **OPPOSITE PAGE:** Kylie, Kody and Kassie dressed at Christmas at the Clark's cottage in Kingston.

TOP: Wendel enjoys a moment with his replica Cobra sports car. **ABOVE:** Ken Daniels interviews Wendel at the Molson Indy race in Toronto. **OPPOSITE PAGE TOP:** NHL All-Star at the Turks and Caicos: (left to right) Dave McIlwain, Wendel, Dave Ellett, Darryl Shannon and Glenn Anderson. **OPPOSITE PAGE BOTTOM:** The Clark family playing hockey on their farm in King City, Ont.

AN EVENI
MOULIN
UGE
TORONTO
EAST GENERAL
HOSPITAL
Foundation
Ou-la-la!
FRIDAY OCTOBER 25, 2002

Wendel and Denise enjoy getting dressed up for social outings with friends or going to events that benefit local charities.

TOP: Wendel, his two daughters and son, along with his parents, gather for Kerry's graduation from the Police Academy. **RIGHT:** Wendel's Mom and Dad and Kylie, Kody and Kassie at Grandparents Day at Country Day School in 2008. This is the last photo of Wendel's Dad that was added to their family scrapbooks.

ABOVE: Wendel and his brother, Kerry, enjoy a reunion. **RIGHT:** Doug Gilmour (left), Bob Rouse and Wendel at the opening of Planet Hollywood in downtown Toronto.

TOP: Kody and Wendel practice driving the boat while on vacation at the Clark's cottage in Kingston. **BELOW LEFT:** Kylie and her Dad in Toronto, 1996. **BELOW RIGHT:** Kassie and Wendel at the cottage in Kingston.

Wendel and the kids always have fun at their lake house on Lake Rosseau in Muskoka, Ont.

ABOVE: Wendel's ice rink at his King City, Ont., farm is used for corporate events throughout the year. **LEFT:** Wendel was the last player cut on the 1987 Team Canada Squad. **OPPOSITE PAGE TOP:** Actor Dan Aykroyd and Wendel enjoy a few laughs togther. **OPPOSITE PAGE BOTTOM:** At a Las Vegas charity event, Wendel poses with TV actress Tiffani-Amber Theissen (middle) and Chris Drury (right) of the Buffalo Sabres.

OPPOSITE PAGE: Wendel's publicity shot from the Leafs' 1993-94 team photo. **TOP:** Denise and Wendel enjoy an afternoon horseback ride together while visiting Dave and Annie Ellet in Arizona. **RIGHT:** Wendel at a local softball game to benefit charity. **BELOW:** Andrew Jackson (left) coordinates most of Wendel's endorsements and appearances.

TOP: Wendel savors an afternoon of playing golf at the Old Course at St. Andrews, Scotland. **ABOVE:** A group of NHL NHL legends gather for a round of golf at a ClubLink Course in 2006: (left to right) Pete Mahovlich, Bernie Federko, Wendel, Bobby Hull, Rick Vaive, Yvan Cournoyer and Dale Hawerchuk. **RIGHT:** In Fall 2001, Wendel graced the front cover of Ontario Golf News.

WENDEL CLARK NIGHT NOVEMBER 16, 2001

Travelodge Hotel

pgi

WM CANADIAN WASTE A WASTE MANAGEMENT COMPANY

PARTSOURCE The Parts. The Pros. The Price.

TOP: Wendel is honoured by the Saskatoon Blades in November 2001 where his sweater Number 22 was retired. **RIGHT:** Kody and his Dad enjoy a few moments of family time. **BOTTOM:** Kody at his 4-year-old birthday party.

RIGHT: Wendel and Kody landscaping with their John Deere tractors. **BELOW:** Kylie, Kassie and Wendel on a pumpkin-hunting trip on a farm. **BOTTOM:** Kylie and her Dad take a ride on the big tractor at the farm in Kelvington, Sask.

TOP: Kody and Wendel enjoy a break from their chores at the farm in King City, Ont. **BELOW LEFT:** Father and son relax in the dressing room before one of Kody's hockey games. **BELOW LEFT:** Wendel and Kody at a mid-winter autographing session in downtown Toronto.

TOP: Denise and Wendel brave the winter chill to celebrate New Year's 2001. **BELOW LEFT:** The Clarks take the ice at the Air Canada Centre for the Maple Leafs' annual Christmas party in 2003. **BELOW RIGHT:** Hosting a friend's wedding at their cottage in Kingston, Ont.

RIGHT: Denise and Wendel pose for an Ad in Canada Living magazine. **BELOW:** Enjoying a fun boat ride at their cottage in Kingston. **BOTTOM:** The Clarks en route to the Bell Gala.

TOP: Kassie (left) and Kylie on their first day of school in 2002. **RIGHT:** Kassie and Kylie (right) at the Aurora Skating Carnival in Aurora, Ont. **BELOW:** Kassie (left) and Kylie in Chicago in 2000.

TOP: The kids and Toby, the pet dog, at Christmas in 2007. **LEFT:** (left to right) Kylie, Kody and Kassie at home in Kingview Acres in King City, Ont. **BELOW:** (left to right) Kylie, Kody and Kassie in Fall 2006.

TOP: Doug Gilmour (left) and Wendel celebrate winning the 1992-93 Norris Division championship. **ABOVE:** (left to right) Dave Ellett, Wendel and Beeker at Wendel's Kingston Cottage in 2002. **RIGHT:** (left to right) Kelly Chase, Wendel, Don Meehan, Gerry Valad and Daryl Lubiniecki enjoy a duck hunting trip.

TOP LEFT: The Clark kids prior to their first day at Country Day School in 2007. **TOP RIGHT:** (left to right) Kassie, Kylie and Kody pose for a Christmas 1999 photo in Chicago. **BOTTOM:** Christmas 2006: The Clark's are joined by Denise's parents, Vern (lower left, holding Kody) and Bettie (lower right); Denise's brother, Calvin Anger and his son, Christopher (top right); and daughter, Alanna Anger (first row, middle).

TOP: Clark family Christmas in Chicago, 1999. **ABOVE:** The Clarks and their new puppy, Toby, at Christmas 2008. **RIGHT:** The Clarks pose for a photo prior to leaving for a Toronto Leafs game which was a tribute to Wendel in 2001.

TOP: Wendel's birthday in 1999, blowing out candles on the cake with Kylie (left) and Kassie. **LEFT:** Wendel and Denise with the two girls at a skating party in Tampa in 1998. **BOTTOM:** The Clarks in Toronto, Fall 1997.

TOP: Kody practicing in the kitchen of the Clark's home in King City, Ont. **BELOW LEFT:** On Halloween 2006 Kody dressed up as a Leafs' version of Scooby Doo. **BELOW RIGHT:** Kody tries on his Dad's first hockey helmet and gloves.

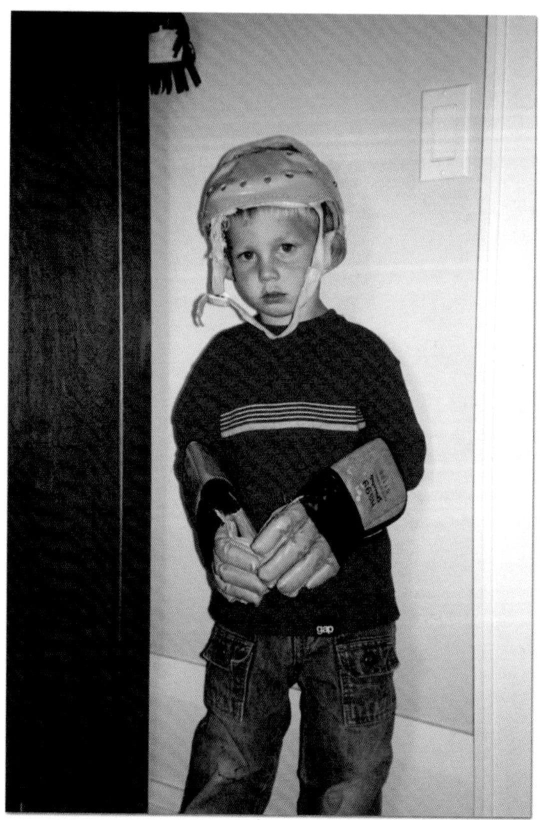

Scott Morrison

Jeff Jackson

Scott Morrison, the recipient of the Hockey Hall of Fame's 2006 Elmer Ferguson Memorial Award, has been covering hockey for 28 years. The Toronto native began his career at The Toronto Sun in 1979. After spending more than 11 years as a hockey writer and columnist at The Toronto Sun, Morrison became the newspaper's sports editor in 1991 and led the section to being named one of North America's top-ten sports sections in 1999, the first sports section in Canada to receive the AP Sports Editors North American Award.

A former two-term president of the Professional Hockey Writers' Association, Scott joined Rogers Sportsnet in 2001 as Managing Editor, Hockey, and is currently both a commentator on "Hockey Night in Canada" and a columnist for CBC.ca.

Scott has written numerous hockey books, including *Hockey Night in Canada: By The Numbers, From 00 to 99* and *Hockey Night in Canada: My Greatest Day*. He resides in Toronto with his son, Mark.

Jeff Jackson was a second-round draft choice of the Toronto Maple Leafs, 28th overall, in the 1983 NHL Draft. The native of Dresden, Ontario, played in 269 NHL games with the Maple Leafs, Rangers, Nordiques and Blackhawks. He also played for Canada's gold medal winning team in the 1985 World Junior Hockey Championship in Helsinki, Finland.

Currently the Assistant General Manager and Director of Hockey Operations for the Toronto Maple Leaf Hockey Club, Jackson also serves as the General Manager and Governor of the Toronto Marlies, the American Hockey League affiliate of the Maple Leafs. Prior to joining the Maple Leafs' front office, Jackson practiced entertainment and sports law for eight years with the firm of Heenan Blaikie LLP in Toronto.

Jeff and his wife, Lara, reside in Burlington, Ontario with their children, Savanna, Liam, Owen and Luke.

For more information on Wendel's golf tournament, appearances and signed memorabilia, please visit:

WWW.WENDELCLARK.CA